American Hea[rt]
True Stories Told in Scenes and Monologues

Written by

Sandra Fenichel Asher
David Barr III
Robert Bella
Joyce Simmons Cheeka
Charlotte P. Chorpenning
Lynne Conner
James DeVita
Steven Dietz
Attilio Favorini
Werdna Phillips Finley
D.W. Gregory
Dan Gutman
Lee Hunkins
Stephen Karam
Carol Korty
Carson Kreitzer
Anne Ludlum
Anne V. McGravie

Ramón Menéndez
Tom Musca
John Neihardt
Martha Hill Newell
Dwight Okita
PJ Paparelli
Nicholas A. Patricca
Paul Peditto
Christopher Sergel
Laura Annawyn Shamas
Charles Smith
James Still
Mamie Till-Mobley
Ilga Katais-Paeglis Vise
Deborah Wicks La Puma
Karen Zacarías
David Zak

Compiled and edited by
Sandra Fenichel Asher

Dramatic Publishing Company
Woodstock, Illinois • Australia • New Zealand • South Africa

*** NOTICE ***

The amateur and stock acting rights to this work are controlled exclusively by THE DRAMATIC PUBLISHING COMPANY, INC., without whose permission in writing no performance of it may be given. Royalty must be paid every time a play is performed whether or not it is presented for profit and whether or not admission is charged. A play is performed any time it is acted before an audience. Current royalty rates, applications and restrictions may be found at our website: www.dramaticpublishing.com, or we may be contacted by mail at: THE DRAMATIC PUBLISHING COMPANY, INC., 311 Washington St., Woodstock, IL 60098.

COPYRIGHT LAW GIVES THE AUTHOR OR THE AUTHOR'S AGENT THE EXCLUSIVE RIGHT TO MAKE COPIES. This law provides authors with a fair return for their creative efforts. Authors earn their living from the royalties they receive from book sales and from the performance of their work. Conscientious observance of copyright law is not only ethical, it encourages authors to continue their creative work. This work is fully protected by copyright. No alterations, deletions or substitutions may be made in the work without the prior written consent of the publisher. No part of this work may be reproduced or transmitted in any form or by any means, electronic or mechanical, including photocopy, recording, videotape, film, or any information storage and retrieval system, without permission in writing from the publisher. It may not be performed either by professionals or amateurs without payment of royalty. All rights, including, but not limited to, the professional, motion picture, radio, television, videotape, foreign language, tabloid, recitation, lecturing, publication and reading, are reserved.

For performance of any songs, music and recordings mentioned in this play which are in copyright, the permission of the copyright owners must be obtained or other songs and recordings in the public domain substituted.

©MMXIV by
DRAMATIC PUBLISHING

Printed in the United States of America
All Rights Reserved
(AMERICAN HEARTBEAT:
TRUE STORIES TOLD IN SCENES AND MONOLOGUES)

ISBN: 978-1-58342-960-0

IMPORTANT BILLING AND CREDIT REQUIREMENTS

All producers of the play *must* give credit to the author of the play in all programs distributed in connection with performances of the play and in all instances in which the title of the play appears for purposes of advertising, publicizing or otherwise exploiting the play and/or a production. The name of the author *must* also appear on a separate line, on which no other name appears, immediately following the title, and *must* appear in size of type not less than fifty percent (50%) the size of the title type. Biographical information on the author, if included in the playbook, may be used in all programs. *In all programs this notice must appear:*

"Produced by special arrangement with
THE DRAMATIC PUBLISHING COMPANY, INC., of Woodstock, Illinois."

Duets: Male **56**
    Free Man of Color 57
    Keeping Mr. Lincoln 59
    The Radiance of a Thousand Suns: The Hiroshima Project 61
    Jackie & Me 63
    Stand and Deliver 67

Trios **69**
    Indian Captive 70
    Freedom Is My Middle Name 73
    The Rememberer 76
    Radium Girls 78
    Black Elk Speaks 82
    Looking for Roberto Clemente 85
    In the Garden of Live Flowers:
       A Fantasia on the Life and Work of Rachel Carson 88

Other Plays of Interest **91**

Foreword

This anthology is aptly titled *American Heartbeat*. Collectively, it embodies the beating heart of the American individual rather than the public face of the national persona. America is a land of contrast and conflict; in short, it's a place where drama happens.

Historical drama gives a face to a name, a voice to a people, and a memorial to the honored dead. The scenes and monologues in this collection allow young people to see history through the eyes of those who lived it and to share that insight with their peers. By bringing these historical figures to life through reading and performance, these pieces can make the past immediate and compelling for students.

The scenes and monologues that Sandra Fenichel Asher has selected for *American Heartbeat* demonstrate a wide variety of subjects and an excellent balance of themes, periods and cultures. The anthology serves as a window not only to the extensive repertoire of historical plays published by Dramatic Publishing but also to the possibilities of exploring the richness of history through theatre and drama.

In Steven Dietz's award-winning dramatization of Dan Gutman's novel *Jackie & Me*, for instance, a young Caucasian sports fan is able to travel through time and space by holding the baseball card of the player he wants to encounter. Joey Stoshack decides to meet Jackie Robinson so he can write his required essay about a famous African American. However, when Joey works the magic, he gets more than he bargained for, as he finds himself living inside the life of a black bat-boy. From this vantage point, he not only witnesses the first African American player joining Major League Baseball but also experiences first-hand the discrimination that Robinson confronted.

By playing or reading a role in a play, students can likewise empathize with individuals from American history and experience the world through their eyes. History engages young people when they develop a kinship with a person who lived it, and reading, performing and watching historical scenes can help them to forge such links.

Staged Readings

While middle- or high-school drama students can be expected to memorize lines and physicalize their characterization, students in a social studies or history class might be better served by presenting staged readings of scenes in this collection.

To present staged readings, students would need to familiarize themselves with the lines and practice reading them aloud, but they wouldn't need to memorize them. Students could hold their scripts, or if they could rest them on a desk or music stand, they would be free to physicalize their characters with their postures and gestures, as well as facial expressions.

In a scene with multiple characters, readers could either look at one another, or look straight forward toward the audience, but say their lines as if speaking to the other actor(s) in the scene. In this manner, the audience can clearly see the expressive faces of the readers. All readers could stand, or they could use chairs or a table to align themselves in an appropriate stage picture. Consider having the readers create a tableau of the scene before they begin so the student audiences can better imagine what the action would look like on stage. Period costumes are not necessary for staged readings. Neutral-colored street clothes and binders containing the script may give the presentation a more polished look.

Student Research

The pieces in *American Heartbeat* feature a few historical individuals whose names would be familiar to almost every secondary school student, such as Abraham Lincoln and Jackie Robinson. Other historical characters were famous figures in their own day, such as poet Philis Wheatley, actress Fannie Kemble and singer Marian Anderson, but are less well known today. However, the majority of historical characters in the collection will be introduced to readers and audience members through the plays themselves.

These lesser-known characters from American history can provide students with a personal connection that will motivate them to do their own research to discover more about these characters and the periods in which they lived. In *Jackie & Me,* Joey Stoshack has little interest, at first, in writing a report on a famous African American until he finds someone on the list of individuals suggested by his teacher who shared his passion for baseball. Likewise, other students who might have an interest in Native American history or the history of aviation might well be stimulated to read the role of Santee chief Little Crow or aviatrix Amelia Earhart and research that individual's life with interest and fervor.

The historical characters revealed in these plays are based on the playwrights' research of actual persons, rather than being fictional creations or composite characters that the playwrights have placed in authentic settings. Because of this, in order to enrich their presentations, students could research the historical individuals and find out more about them before they present their scenes and monologues in class.

While the events are historical and most of the characters are based on actual people, it is important for students to understand that playwrights present them in a way that is engaging for their audience. Just as William Shakespeare condensed events in his history plays to make the stories more compelling, some of the playwrights who have contributed to this collection have abridged, condensed, combined and intensified events in American history in order to make the stories more stage-worthy. It might be stimulating to have students write essays that compare and contrast how an event is portrayed in the drama with how it is rendered in historical accounts and other renditions of the event.

The scenes could also help students to appreciate the different sources from which historical representations are drawn. For example, one scene was reproduced from the actual transcription of a conversation between a 911 dispatcher and a teacher. For several of the plays, the playwrights interviewed people who appear as characters in the plays, and the scripts closely follow the content of the interviews. Other dramas in the collection are based upon journals written by participants in or witnesses of the dramatized events. In some cases, when the record of the historical event being portrayed was less complete, the playwright took liberties in filling out the details. These differences can help students understand how history is researched and composed in history books and how the historical event is adapted to reach live audiences.

Cross-Curricular Collaboration

As a high-school drama teacher, I often connected my school's social studies classes with my in-class projects and productions. For example, we presented a staged reading of *Black Elk Speaks* for an American history class when they were studying Western expansion. We had an insightful post-reading discussion involving myself, my drama students, the social studies students and their teacher about the differences between the portrayal of Native American tribes in their history text and the portrayal they had witnessed in the theatrical reading.

The cross-curricular experience can also enrich student participation when historical plays receive full production support. Nathan Criman, who teaches drama at Mountain View High School in Orem, Utah, has used his theatre productions to reinforce themes explored in other academic classes in order to make learning more relevant for the students. His drama students present scenes in social studies and language arts classes to build student interest in attending the full performances. He also involves drama and history students in researching the visual record of the pertinent period and in selecting and compiling images that are projected behind and around the set during those productions.

When Alicia Sanders taught theatre at Oakwood High School in Morgan Hill, Calif., and staged plays of historical and social significance, she engaged in a hybrid learning experience with her social studies colleagues in order for their students to fully understand the significance of the events in the play. Half of her drama students' preparation time was spent blocking and rehearsing, and half their time was spent learning about the historical context that inspired the playwright to write the play. In their social studies classes, these same students watched selected videos and read texts about the time period.

Further Uses of the Anthology

Mr. Criman says that his drama students learn better when they can identify with the characters from the eras that they study. "A book like *American Heartbeat*," he said, "will help bring history alive for the social studies instructor, assist language arts teachers in demonstrating biographical writing, and aid drama teachers in reaching students who wish to act realistically. This text could be used as a school-wide, multi-subject sourcebook that would encourage cross-curricular collaboration while costing much less than other academic materials."

Ms. Sanders endorses the book as a source of monologues, noting "we are always hunting for unique pieces that help our students understand a variety of characters." Her school also holds a "freedom festival" and she envisions using some of the pieces in the book as part of that presentation.

Ms. Sanders also notes that the collection would be helpful for both drama and social studies teachers as they implement new state and national standards. "In this modern era, education is putting a greater emphasis on the understanding and inclusion of nonfiction. Dramatic texts that pull from historical sources are extremely powerful and can be beneficial in a social studies classroom as well as in a drama classroom. The variety of perspectives represented in this text is compelling, and as a theatre teacher I am instantly drawn to these pieces. They offer fresh and unique approaches to understanding deeply rooted societal truths and historical moments, and I am enthusiastic about using them in my classroom."

Themed Presentations

There are a number of other themes and motifs that recur in the pieces in this collection around which presentations could be centered. Several of the pieces in the collection put a face on labor issues, others explore the underground railroad and the Civil Rights era. Some examine the pursuit of the "American Dream," while a few provide glimpses of American presidents in more private moments. Some of the plays highlight chapters in American history that deserve student scrutiny, such as the creation and detonation of the atom bomb and the suppression of Native American culture in the conquest of the American West.

It should be noted that, while these dramatic excerpts present excellent acting opportunities for adolescents, some of the plays represented in this volume were originally written for adult actors to perform for adult audiences. A few of the plays contain graphic descriptions of violent events in history that might disturb young readers and actors. I would therefore encourage teachers to read the full scripts themselves, when practical, so they can help to contextualize the events for their students and discuss their treatment in the dramas.

As a high-school teacher, I found that my drama students had limited interest in history until they performed dramas set in historical periods. Doing so made the past seem present and their ancestors seem intriguing. Acting historical scenes and playing historical characters let my students see that young people in the past faced many of the same challenges as they face now, and some that young people no longer have to encounter. Enacting history helps students see themselves as players in the ongoing drama of American life and to experience history as if they were there.

John Dilworth Newman, Ph.D.
Utah Valley University

American Heartbeat:
True Stories Told in Scenes and Monologues

Monologues: Female

Shame the Devil!
An Audience With Fanny Kemble
By Anne Ludlum

In this one-woman play based on a true story, famed Shakespearean actress Fanny Kemble tells the audience about her marriage to a man who, much to her surprise and dismay, turned out to be a slave-owner. Here, she describes an experience on his plantation on the Sea Islands of Georgia in the 1830s.

***

FANNY. There are four "camps" on the island, each consisting of a dozen or so cabins and a cook's shop where the daily rations are boiled in a huge cauldron.

(FANNY "enters a cabin" from UR.)

I called at one of the cabins. It was a mere wooden frame, pinned to the earth by a brick chimney. I entered the single room. It was about twelve by fifteen feet, with two tiny cupboards for sleeping. Two families—two large families, one of seven people and one of ten people—resided in it. There were no chairs nor table, no furniture of any kind. Rags, shavings, chickens, filth littered the floor.

A group of half-naked children, all with babies on their backs, cowered around two or three cinders. When the mothers are in the field, the older children act as "little nursies." They watch over the babies and carry them to the mothers to be nourished.

I bade these "little nursies" tend the fire and sweep the floor. Then I set myself to expelling the poultry.

(FANNY "shoos" with her skirt.)

Shoo-chick! Shoo-chick! Shoo-chick! Chick-chick-chick-chick! Shoo-shoo-shoo!

The children burst into laughter at me, but then they fell to imitating me.

(FANNY crosses to DC.)

I proclaimed to all the "little nursies" that I would give one cent to every child whose baby's face should be clean and one cent more to every individual with clean face—and hands—of his or her own. My appeal was fully comprehended by the majority. Subsequently, when ever I emerged from my front door, I was surrounded by swarms of children—their little charges on their backs—all with shining, and in many cases still wet, faces and hands. Thus did I ingeniously introduce hygiene onto the island.

(FANNY starts to cross to bookcase; stops.)

As well as bribery and corruption.

A Midnight Cry:
The Underground Railroad to Freedom

By James DeVita
Musical selections and arrangements by Josh Schmidt
Additional selections and arrangements by Sheri Williams Panell

Lida Anderson is a determined and courageous 17-year-old who escapes slavery through the Underground Railroad. Secretly taught to read by her Uncle Eli, she recalls the joy of recognizing a written word for the first time.

***

LIDA *(shift)*. I 'members the first time I read a word. So scared my fingers barely hold the book 'cause the mastah always be tellin' us learnin' jus' 'bout the worst sin in the world. The first word, jus' a tiny word, but the fear in me was a yellin' that if I go 'n say it out loud the ground jus' might open up 'n swallow me whole; or the lightnin' goin' to strike me down and dere be nuthin' left o' po' little Lida Anderson but a itty-bitty spot o' ash. But, I tell you, my mind run further away by saying that one word then my body ever did. *(Sounding out the word.)* "The." *(Sounding out letters.)* T-H-E. "The." Tha's right. Tha's all it was. Be better if it was a bit mo' interestin' word. Like the first word I ever read was *freedom*, o' *faith*, o' *hope*. That make fo' some fine readin' maybe. But I didn't read those words. I read "the." But I read it. I read it ma'self. 'N the ground didn't swallow me up, 'n lightin' didn't stike, 'n those three little do-nuthin' letters had more hope, faith, 'n freedom in 'em than anythin' I ever known. They teach me that things jus' been kept *away* from me. And once a body learn that there's things that belong to *everyone*, but only some peoples have 'em and somes don't—why, then the world ain't never be the same fo' you. Freedom like that. Freedom a thing some peoples have and somes don't, but it belong to everyone. It like the air. Ain't nobody own the air. A thing can't be mo' wrong than that.

Amelia Lives

By Laura Annawyn Shamas

Aviation pioneer Amelia Earhart tells her own story in this one-woman play set during her last flight in July of 1937. In this excerpt, she describes the evening she received the National Geographic Society's Special Gold Medal for her extraordinary accomplishments.

***

AMELIA. I found a very formal gown, the kind I had always wanted to wear, at least once, for the fun of it. Long, white, a low-cut neckline ... It is a new me. It's an Amelia that I like, an Amelia who can do what she wants, an Amelia who can succeed. I received the National Geographic Society's Special Gold Medal. In the speech before the presentation, it is mentioned that not only am I the first woman to cross the Atlantic by air, I am the first to cross it alone, the only person in the world to cross it twice, and the first woman to receive the Society's Gold Medal. Thunderous applause rang through Constitution Hall. Is it for me that these people are cheering? Is it because of me that they received 10,000 requests to attend this presentation? When President Hoover praised a woman who "has made all mankind her debtor by her demonstration of new possibilities of the human spirit and the human will," was he talking about me? During the applause, I hear cries of "Earhart! Earhart!" so I know that this dream is real ... They beckon me to the podium.

(She motions for the applause to end. She smiles graciously.)

"Thank you. Thank you very much."

(She takes box from prop box and holds it, showing a gold medaL)

"This is wonderful."

(She motions to all of them.)

"This is wonderful. But this honor is too great for my feat because my flight has added nothing to the science of aviation. Indeed, my adventure just proved how far this science has already progressed. My flight has received a great deal of recognition, and there have been many stories told about it. If you had paid attention to all of the rumors, I'm sure you would not have awarded me this medal. But for the record, and I must add, against the advice of my husband, I would like to quickly clear up a few of the misconceptions that have been brought to my attention about the solo flight. First of all, I did not land within six feet of a hedge of trees. Moreover, I hope everyone here realizes that I did not damage that kind Irishman's roof—I landed in his pasture. And there was no dead cow involved, unless one died of fright upon seeing me for the first time. But I saw no dead cow and that kind farmer never mentioned it to me. Finally, I did have considerably more than one gallon of gasoline left in my tank. There's even proof of that. Ask the Irish government—they made me pay taxes on 100 gallons."

(She pauses, showing a serious transition.)

"Seriously, I must pay considerable tribute to Bernt Balchem, my advisor on this flight. In my opinion, any expedition owes sixty percent of its success to the preparation beforehand. Flying by instruments is a great step forward for aviation, and I hope that the flight has meant something to women in aviation. If it has, I shall feel justified; but I can't claim anything else … Thank you."

(She stops, changes her position, making it clear that the speech is over. She holds up the medal in the light before putting it away.)

My very own gold medal.

Walking Toward America

By Sandra Fenichel Asher
Adapted from the memoirs of Ilga Katais-Paeglis Vise.

Driven from their Latvian homeland during World War II, Ilga and her parents walk 500 miles across Germany to safety. In this play, one actor portrays Ilga from child to grandparent, plus all the other characters in her story. Here, Ilga recreates her family's arrival in America in 1952.

***

ILGA. Slowly, we steam into New York Bay, toward Manhattan. The skyline looms before us. Even in daytime, there are lights everywhere—in windows, around the harbor, across the bridges. No blackout here! *(Beat.)* The ship docks. Noise and commotion. Passport checks. *(Mimes picking up her bundle and suitcase.)* Baggage collection. Custom controls. Another line. Another booth. Then … $5 awarded to each of us! *(Beat. Puts down her bundle and suitcase, paces anxiously.)* Someone from Church World Service will meet us. This is what I waited for, longed for, in refugee camp. Yes, we were safe and warm and dry. Yes, we were fed every day. But years passed while Papa went on believing Latvia would be free of Russians and we could go home. The Lacis family went to America. My friends from the camp school went to America. We wrote letters to one another! *(Beat, then confidentially.)* One day, while Mama and Papa were away, working in their rented garden plot, an American representative came by. I signed us up. *(Beat, then impatiently.)* Still, another year passed before a sponsor was found. Then examinations and inoculations and papers and more waiting—

CHURCH WORLD SERVICE LADY *(reading loudly from a list, searching for a response)*. MR. AND MRS. KATAIS … ? MR. AND MRS. KRAUKLIS … ?

(Beat. ILGA looks about, then spots the CHURCH WORLD SERVICE LADY.)

ILGA. At last! The Church World Service lady!

CHURCH WORLD SERVICE LADY *(loudly and slowly, over-enunciating each word in her earnest desire to be understood)*. YOU WILL TAKE THE FERRY TO THE JERSEY SIDE, THEN A TRAIN TO CHICAGO.

JANIS. Chicago? The gangster city? Al Capone?

CHURCH WORLD SERVICE LADY. YOUR SPONSOR IS NEAR CHICAGO.

JANIS. Not New York? I would rather go back to Germany.

ZENTA. Jani! I am not getting on that ship again!

CHURCH WORLD SERVICE LADY. NOT CHICAGO, NEAR CHICAGO. OAK … LAWN … ILL … IN … OY.

JANIS *(with difficulty, he's speaking English now, but also with a hint of mischievous mimicking).* Ill … in … oy? Ilga! What … did they … teach you … in refugee camp … about Ill … in … noy?

ILGA. They grow corn … and hogs.

JANIS *(thoughtfully).* Hogs?

ILGA. Papa has little English. He is catching only the last word of things. Chicago! Illinois! Hogs! But "hogs" seems to calm him. We know hogs. *(Beat.)* It is already night when we follow the Church World Service lady to the ferry and cross the Hudson River. Its dark waters reflect the lights of Manhattan. What a wonder it all is!

CHURCH WORLD SERVICE LADY. IN TWO HOURS, YOU TAKE THE TRAIN TO CHICAGO. WELCOME TO AMERICA!

ILGA. She hands over the tickets, and then leaves. *(Puts down her bundle and suitcase.)* We are alone in the vast train station … the "K families" … Katais and Krauklis … alone … except for the hundreds of people rushing past. *(Beat, sniffs the air.)* A delicious aroma drifts toward us from a market stand with colorful light bulbs strung all around. *(Edging closer to read.)* Hot. Dogs. Twenty-five cents.

ZENTA. They do not eat dogs here … do they?

ILGA. We watch people rush up to the counter and speak to the burly man wearing a white apron and a little white sailor hat. Tongs in hand, he grabs a steaming item from a pot, tosses it into something he holds in his other hand, then wraps and delivers it to the customer. *(Watches a customer pass by.)* A sausage!

JANIS *(frowns at the strange bills in his hand).* We have this … money …

(Beat. JANIS is confused as to how to proceed, then he urges ILGA to take the bills.)

JANIS *(cont'd).* You speak better English, Ilga. You can order.

ILGA *(takes charge, sensing a reversal in their roles).* It is all right, Papa. I can do it. *(Gathers the money and steps up to the hot dog stand. Then, with excitement and bravado.)* Twelve!

HOT DOG VENDOR. For you?

ILGA. Yes!

HOT DOG VENDOR. Mustard? Catsup? Pickle relish?

ILGA. He points to spigots dripping red and yellow. He picks up a ladle brimming with something green. I have never seen such bright colors! *(To HOT DOG VENDOR, vigorously shaking her head.)* NO!

(Beat. Then she hands over the money, takes change, examines it for a moment with curiosity, pockets it and passes out hot dogs to her group. She takes a bite, and smiles broadly, nodding at the others in approval.)

ILGA *(cont'd)*. Standing in a circle together, we beam at one another as we munch down each tasty morsel. *(Beat. Finishes her hot dog and wipes her mouth.)* Our first real American food.

The Face of Emmett Till

By Mamie Till-Mobley and David Barr III

August, 1955. Emmett Louis Till, a black teenager from Chicago, is abducted, tortured and murdered while visiting relatives in Money, Mississippi. His mother's courage in seeking justice makes this "the hate crime that changed America." This monologue captures her love, grief and determination.

***

MAMIE. Emmett screams, then his screams go away. But the nightmare always comes back. The very next night. Sometimes, that same night. *(Beat.)* Mama, I feel like I'm going crazy.

[ALMA. *It's a wonder we all ain't lost our minds over this thing.*]

The thing is, I get up every morning. I brush my teeth, wash my face. I fix my hair and dress. And then ... I could just kill myself for not protecting him better. For not ... being the kind of mother who would always keep her child safe. *(Beat.)* When I found out I was pregnant ... I dreamed of graduations, a wedding, someone to take care of me when I got old. Even grandchildren. Now ... *(Brief pause.)* I keep thinking about all the things he'll *miss*. All the things ... *I'll* miss. *(Beat.)* He'll never graduate from high school. *(Beat.)* He'll never drive a car ... or go to prom. *(Beat.)* He'll never fall in love ... or get his heart broken. *(Beat.)* My little boy ... will never have children. To raise in his image. *(Beat.)* I heard one time ... that when a child dies ... he disappears into the blank pages of his potential. All they could have become. Everything they might have accomplished.

[ALMA. *I just...can't believe he's gone.*]

The other day, I saw an ad in the newspaper talking about this new movie ... I can't remember the name of it right now. Something with Humphrey Bogart in it, I think. And ... the first thing I thought was ... I've got to make sure I tell Emmett about this movie. He always loved *Bogie. (Long pause.)* I suppose, when you lose a child ... everything stirs up old memories. *(Beat.)* I'm just thirty-three years old, Mama. And I'm coming to the realization ... that this is something ... I'll have to live with for the rest of my life. *(Beat.)* Emmett ... is not coming back to me. I realize that ... *right now*. Tomorrow, I might have a harder time accepting it. But his death ... and the *way that he died* ... it's ...

oh … how can I explain it … *(Pause.) It's mine now.* It's … a part of me. *It's inside … of me. (Pause. Fighting back tears.)* I miss me, Mama. *I miss me.* I miss the way I was … the way *we were. (Beat.)* Everyone keeps tellin' me that it's going to be all right. But … I'm just not whole anymore. I am not … *Mamie* anymore. And sometimes … sometimes, Mama … I just miss *me. (Long pause.)* I'm going to the trial.

Ev'ry Time I Feel the Spirit

By David Barr III

World-renowned contralto Marian Anderson wants to be recognized for her artistry, and she is, but her struggles and accomplishments as a black woman throughout her long career hold great social significance as well. In this scene, she and a companion are passing through Virginia on a southbound train in 1929.

***

YOUNGER MARIAN. The first time I toured the South, I took my mother with me. We got off the train in Montgomery and … this very smartly dressed white lady rushed over to meet us. She told the man who was with us … who just so happened to be white … that his room was ready and waiting at the hotel. Then she turned to us and said, "Marian, you're going to stay with the Robinsons. They have a nice clean house. You'll just love it there."

[BILLY (an empathetic chuckle to himself). Oh yes.]

Well … she wanted to leave my manager at the hotel but he insisted on seeing our accommodations. When we drove through the Negro section of town the white lady saw me leaning forward and looking around at the crowded, depressed surroundings: houses that badly needed repair and paint, old women sitting on their wooden stoops … children playing in the front yards … that were just dust really. And I'll never forget … she said, "Marian, your people just love it here. They're so much happier down here than anywhere else." Now, my manager was sitting beside her … in the front seat. So she turns to him and starts to explain that … "I was just telling Marian how much better off the Nigras are down here, where we love them and take care of them." *(BILLY, laughing, shaking his head, again chuckling to himself. Still drinking his Chivas. They both laugh. Pause.)* The greatest thrill in my life was to make enough money to call my mother's store manager one morning and say … "I'm sorry, Miss Hennessy, but my mother won't be coming to work today … or any other day."

Monologues: Male

Free Man of Color

By Charles Smith

It's 1824, and the president of Ohio University has brought John Newton Templeton to Ohio to be the first freed slave to attend the college. Though Ohio is a free state, Templeton cannot be housed with white students and so lives in the president's home as a "student servant." The complexities of Templeton's position are evident in this excerpt.

***

JOHN *(to audience)*. Sure enough, the next day, a wagon rolled through town with a washboard jug band on the back. The band played music announcing to anyone who didn't already know that that the circus had officially come to town. The same day that wagon rolled into town, Reverend Wilson rolled out of town. Said he had to meet with some men in Chillicothe but I thought the real reason was that he didn't want to be here when the circus arrived. The circus consisted of an assortment of wonderful oddities and delights. There was a man who had six fingers on each hand, a woman who was covered with hair from head to toe, and a boy who could twist himself into all kinds of unnatural-looking shapes. And of course, they had the women who did trick horseback riding, bareback and saddled. They also had an elephant, a lion, a zebra that they called a striped horse, and an ostrich that caused a lot of excitement. I don't think anybody had ever seen a seven-foot bird before. I think a whole lot of folks wanted to eat it. But by far, the most popular attraction, the one thing that amazed young and old alike, was Mongo, the Trained Ape. Mongo was an ape who had been trained to perform various tricks. He drank water from a cup. He smoked a cigar. He sat at a table, and when it came time to eat, he used a spoon. This was a particularly remarkable feat, especially when you consider that at least half of the population of town at the time did not use or even own a spoon. But the most disconcerting part of this animal's act was that they had outfitted him with a hat, shirt with a collar, and pair of trousers. Mongo attracted fairly moderate attention for almost a week. But this was nothing like the sensation caused later when, late one night, somebody sneaked into the encampment and defaced the board that stood in front of Mongo's tent. To the shock of some, and to the delight of others, on the board announcing Mongo the Trained Ape, somebody had crossed out the name Mongo and had written, in its place, John Newton Templeton.

The Remembererer

By Steven Dietz
Based on the unpublished memoir As My Sun Now Sets *by Joyce Simmons Cheeka, as told to Werdna Phillips Finley*

The year is 1911, and young Native Americans are being taken from their families by force to be "re-educated" in government boarding schools. Transferred from one school to another, troubled teenager Darin Longfeather is asked what he did that resulted in a beating at his former school.

***

DARIN LONGFEATHER. Do you want to know what I did? DO YOU? *(Pause, softer now.)* I said my mother's name. At night, in my sleep, I said my mother's name. And they heard me. "NO INDIAN NAMES," they said, "NO INDIAN NAMES." So, the next night, they made me sleep on the wood floor, without a blanket. And they watched me. And, I closed my eyes and I tried with all my heart to forget my mother's name. But, in my sleep, I said it again. So, the next night they took me to the barn. And they stuffed cloth in my mouth. And, they all stood around me while I slept. I tried to stay awake. I tried not to think about her, or her face, or her voice. I tried to pretend my mother was dead. But, in the middle of the night, they woke me up and tied my hands to a post. They told me I'd said her name again in my sleep. And I swore I'd never do it again but they said it was too late. That I would have to be taught a lesson. *(Pause.)* They took off my shirt. *(Pause.)* One of the men took off his belt. *(Pause.)* And he started hitting me. *(Pause. Very distant sound of leather striking flesh.)* And I didn't cry. Because I could hear my mother's voice, saying: You'll be home soon, my beautiful boy. *(Pause, softly.)* You'll be home soon.

Sounds of Silents (The Essanay Years)

By Paul Peditto

The move from Chicago to California in the early years of film-making opens up new possibilities and offers new challenges. Silent film pioneer G.M. "Bronco Billy" Anderson solves one problem—and prolongs his own career—by creating a new phenomenon, the "stunt double."

***

ANDERSON. Do I look stupid? I mean entirely stupid? I got a problem I can't figure out. The Old West is dying. We got expert horsemen, I'm saying hell-for-leather cowboys with ten years topping off broncs out of work. Famous men like Sourdough Johnson and the Wyoming Kid, useless as Conestoga wagons! Well damn, I hate to see that! My problem is the plains. The open plains. Broncho Billy can ride at breakneck speeds he never could in Chicago! He can rescue a moving buckboard! Or fight hand to hand on speeding horses where one slip means serious injury or death! Or take a fall … off a cliff … after riding through a burning forest! To which, to all of which I say: No, thank you! Why take the risk? Deprive my fans and the movie-going public of their hero Broncho Billy!? No sir, I refuse to be that selfish! But what to do? When it hits me. "Say Sourdough, say Wyoming, c'mon over here! I'm gonna fix y'all up. I want you boys to fall off some horses for me, do a few other stunts, I'll give ya $3.20 a day and all the whiskey you can drink!" These fellas never made more than thirty bucks for a month of eighteen-hour days. They know I'm a dime-store cowboy, but they love me. I invent a thing called a "stunt double." For the good of the public, you see? All so's Broncho Billy can promise the pretty schoolmarm the rustlers didn't hurt him one little bit when they pitched him forty feet into that canyon! Up, up, Pinto. And away!

Looking Over the President's Shoulder

By James Still

As a butler in the White House from 1931 to 1952, Alonzo Fields has weathered the changes wrought and demands made by both Republican and Democratic administrations. In this one-man play, he takes us behind the scenes to show us presidents, first ladies, families and guests as he knew them.

***

ALONZO FIELDS. "Dinner is served, Mr. President."

Often, we had two afternoon teas ... four hundred people at four o'clock and four hundred *more* people at five o'clock. It was really commendable of the first lady to invite so many people from different walks of life. But many of the Washington high society were making catty remarks about "anybody and everybody being invited to the White House ... " One lady said she went to a White House tea and behold—her own maid was in the reception line! This was more than she could stand, so she feigned a sudden illness and left. After years of Republican rule, the Democrats were like people who seldom go out to dinner. A White House invitation had to be proved with some memento ... Linen tea napkins with the U.S. seal disappeared a gross at a time. Spoons disappeared six dozen a tea. Then there was the lady guest who was having trouble closing her bag, so she asked a White House maid if she would fasten the bag for her. The maid discovered a fourteen-inch silver tray given to the White House in 1898 and inscribed "The President's House." The maid asked me what she should do. She said, "Maybe Mrs. Roosevelt gave her the tray." I told her, "I'll take the tray back to the pantry." "But what if she looks in her bag before she leaves and asks about it?" *(Laughing:)* "That lady will never question you about this. Trust me."

Mrs. Roosevelt was so tireless that she assumed everyone else was the same. I don't think she realized there was a difference between working for posterity—and just working to live. Once I went three straight months without a day off and worked thirteen hours a day. It's funny about people ... in any capacity of life—butler, chief butler, bottle washer or president—you seldom hear the compliment "well done." But if something goes wrong—don't worry, you'll soon hear the bad news. I used to say to the gang, "Thanks, girls and boys ... we had a good party. And remember—you're helping to make history"—which would always bring a retort like "OK, Chief. You just keep paying us and we'll let you make the history." My men called me "Chief" or "Fields"—to my face. But behind my back they called me "Donald Duck"—because I was always "quack-quack-quacking" at the staff. We had nicknames for the presidents too. We called President Hoover—"Smiley"—because he seldom did. We called President Roosevelt "Charlie Potatoes"—because back in Indiana we had a grocer who we called Charlie Potatoes—he could sell you anything! So President Roosevelt was Charlie Potatoes. Because of President Truman's outspoken manner we named him "Billie Bunk Full of Spunk." Mrs. Hoover we called "Mother," for she was like my mother—just one look from her told you when you were wrong. We called Mrs. Truman—"Mrs. Truman"—because she wouldn't stand for any foolishness. And Mrs. Roosevelt we called "Alice in Wonderland" for she was always on the go and in a world all her own.

The Radiance of a Thousand Suns: The Hiroshima Project

By Anne V. McGravie, Dwight Okita, Nicholas A. Patricca and David Zak
Music by Chuck Larkin

On August 6, 1945, the first atomic bomb hits its target, the Japanese city of Hiroshima. Those who worked on the bomb's development had been excited to the point of obsession by the process and its many scientific, engineering and logistical challenges. But success brings with it unexpected repercussions.

***

PHYSICIST. We were in a big study hall when we found out. Someone shouted: "It's a boy." That was the security code for a successful explosion. "It's a boy" to signal that the bomb worked; "It's a girl" to signal it didn't. Since I had worked on the timing device, accurate to one millionth of a second, I jumped up and started going wild with my "war whoops." I was ecstatic: maybe you don't understand. It's one thing to successfully explode a stationary atomic bomb, quite another a moving bomb, a bomb that you drop from 20,000 feet from a moving airplane. Champagne appeared magically out of nowhere. One of the physicists had secretly wired the Sangre de Cristo Mountains with fireworks. He threw the switch. It was an incredible display.

Then. all of a sudden, I got very tired. Maybe it was the champagne. I was so glad the war was over. I felt such relief. I went out into the cold desert air, I walked toward the mountains, the Blood of Christ Mountains … for the first time the irony in this name struck this lapsed Catholic.

I started to cry. I never cry. It felt very weird. This great sadness had swelled up inside me: it overflowed into tears. I remembered Trinity: the searing light; the hot blast on my face; the mushroom cloud … I walked further out into the desert. I wondered about the people of Hiroshima. I didn't feel any guilt. I felt something totally beyond guilt. What happens to people when an atomic bomb explodes a hundred feet from their home, a thousand feet, a mile? What happens to people?

I prayed, I don't know to what or for what … but I prayed.

The Love Song of J. Robert Oppenheimer

By Carson Kreitzer

A brilliant physicist whose never-ending thirst for knowledge eventually led to his becoming "the Father of the Atomic Bomb," J. Robert Oppenheimer is far less equipped to deal with the Red Scare that questions his loyalty and threatens to strip him of his security clearance as it sweeps across the United States after World War II.

***

OPPIE. Lying awake at night, I think of…many things. Mostly the critical mass of fissionable material. The critical mass of scientists. Fissionable minds. Will we be able to translate Theory into Practice? In time—?

Sometimes I remember
my mother's hands
smoothing down my hair.
With the soft kidskin gloves she always wore. To cover a…defect in her right hand. It was not fully formed. Missing three fingers.
We never discussed it. It just…was.
Soft gloves touching my face. smoothing down my hair.
Sending me off to Dr. Adler's School for Ethical Culture. *(Smiles.)*

Ethical…Culture.
How young we all were.
To believe in such…possibilities.

[(MOTHER appears. Takes off a large, broad-brimmed picture hat. Takes off one glove. Is about to take off the other. OPPIE turns to see her. She disappears.)]

Once Dr. Adler brought a geologist in to speak to my form. And this man brought with him a great iron contraption, much like a large ice chipper, and a box of unassuming-looking round brown rocks, only slightly larger than a fist.

He rested one carefully in the contraption, brought the handle down with a sharp CRACK, and there lay the geode, in two halves, inner cavern of crystals sparkling in the first light it had ever seen.

I … laughed aloud. With the shock of it. The truth of it.

And I knew. I had got to look harder. To know what was inside things.

Mineralogy was my first love.
It set me on a rather direct path…to here.
Los Alamos.
Where they question my associations. Read my mail.
Listen to every phone call. Listen at the keyhole till I think I will go mad.

Duets: 1 Male, 1 Female

On the Line

By Carol Korty

Factory work in 1912 often meant long hours, low wages and dangerous conditions for employees. The Washington Mill in Lawrence, Massachusetts, is no exception. On a winter's day on Lawrence Common, an Industrial Workers of the World representative and Miss Flanagan, a union member, attempt to mobilize workers to fight for their rights.

IWW LEADER
MISS FLANAGAN

***

IWW LEADER *(using following lines and ad-libs to get whole audience onto their feet)*. Stand over here—join your neighbors—fill the whole Common. Stand close together with your working brothers and sisters. All of you get up on your feet. Stamp them to keep warm. It's much too cold today to sit. See the steam your breath makes in the cold air? It looks like the breath of a dragon—a mighty dragon of workers! The time has come for you to shout "no" to the treatment you have gotten in these mills. To shout "no" to being treated like a dog. To shout "no" to being paid starvation wages. Let's hear these "no's" with one mighty voice.

[CROWD (urged on by ACTORS in character). No! No! No!]

MISS F. What have the owners done for you? Built the mills here? Given you jobs? Was this a kindness to you? No, they put up the money for the factories, but it was you who built them, and it is you who work them. Who makes the cloth that makes the money? But who keeps the money?

[CROWD. The owners.]

MISS F. You get barely enough to pay for your food and rent.

IWW LEADER. Is this justice? They hire you when they want. They fire you when they want. They feel this is their right because they own the mills. But they do not own you. If you do not work, what will they have? How much money does an empty mill make? Does it run without people working it? Your work is your strength. It is real strength. The most powerful force in this country.

[(CROWD ad-libs cheers.)]

IWW LEADER *(cont'd)*. How can you use this strength? Alone you can do nothing. You can not walk up to the overseer and say, "Give me more money." You would not get it, and you would be fired. And, if you are fired, it is easy to hire someone else. There are 80,000 people here in Lawrence. All of us need to work to buy food and clothes, to pay the rent, to send money to families in the old country, to save in the bank for a house. This is good. But, when you think only of getting it for yourself, the bosses have won.

MISS F. Remember those posters showing people carrying bags of gold from the factory to the bank? Where are those bags of gold?

[(CROWD ad-libs responses.)]

MISS F. *(cont'd).* Did the posters show long hours? The accidents that cripple you? Speed of the machines? The heat and noise? Crowded houses and children being sick? Why are your children hungry and in rags? They work in the mills from quarter of seven in the morning until after five at night. When do they see the sun? When do they play? One out of three children dies by the age of twenty! Owners and rich people say work is good for children. Why aren't the bosses sending their children to work alongside yours?

[(CROWD cheers at the irony.)]

IWW LEADER. Many of you here were born outside of America or have parents who were. Why did you come? To be part of a new country where everyone has a chance? Be able to earn a living and have a voice of your own—to live where people make the decisions together, not just one or two at the top. You were told that America was big enough for all of you. And it is. Turks, Irish, Finns, Lithuanians, Africans, Spanish, Portuguese, Greeks. You are all here.

MISS F. Armenians, Germans, Franco-Belgians, South Americans, Syrians, Chinese.

[Note: These were the major ethnic groups in Lawrence in 1912. Add names of additional ethnic groups present in the audience, if known.]

IWW LEADER. Many different national traditions is a great strength. Become members of the union of Industrial Workers of the World because we are members of one great family of workers from all over the world. It is the owners who want to keep you separate from one another. Like this. *(Holds up hand with fingers spread and then pushes down one finger at a time to demonstrate his point.)* But if you can stay together as a fist ... *(Makes a fist.)* ... you cannot be pushed over. Together you have great strength. Together you're a hand that works as one powerful being. Not with violence, because if you are violent, they will bring in the militia to destroy you. But with the power of united workers who choose not to work until conditions are just!

MISS F. Let each national group elect a representative to sit on a central strike committee for all of us. Voice your demands so that everyone is heard. As one body, go out on strike together. As one body, stay out on strike together until the owners listen and give you what you need.

IWW LEADER. Stick together and be powerful.

Radium Girls

By D.W. Gregory

Like so many of her factory co-workers who used radium to paint luminous watch faces in the 1920s, Grace Fryer has fallen ill with a mysterious disease. The fight for her life becomes a fight for justice that changes everything, including her marriage plans.

TOM

GRACE

***

TOM. I'll tell ya what we shoulda done. We shoulda took that reporter up on her offer when we had the chance. That's what we shoulda done.

GRACE. Five thousand dollars. Don't make me laugh.

TOM. We shoulda talked her up too—'cause I'll tell ya what—they'da paid. And I'll tell ya what else we shoulda done—

GRACE. Stop tellin' me what we shoulda done! Lots of things we shoulda done. It don't do no good to think about 'em now.

TOM. All right. Keep your shirt on.

GRACE. What do you think? The red or the blue?

TOM. So what's Berry say? Is he gonna go back to the company?

GRACE. I like the red, but it don't fit so good these days.

TOM. Is he gonna try to talk the company up a bit?

GRACE. Miss Wiley thinks another interview will do the job. So I say, what's one more? Ya know?

TOM. It's worth a try, don't you think? What if they came up to five thousand? Would ya take it then?

GRACE. Let 'em come up. I'm not cavin' in …

TOM. It's called a settlement.

GRACE. A settlement. It's a just a way for them to hide.

TOM. Let 'em hide.

GRACE. Then they win.

TOM. So they win. They're gonna win anyway.

GRACE. Nice you got so much confidence in me.

TOM. Grace, for Christ's sake. You got one lawyer workin' for nothin'— up against six other lawyers who are getting a bundle. And you think you got a chance?

GRACE. Y'know what I found out today? They put lead screens in the laboratory. For the technicians. Did they give us lead screens?

TOM. Oh Jesus.

GRACE. Whatd'ya think? One hundred girls in a room and they're gonna spend that kinda money on us?

TOM. Grace—

GRACE. And they want to keep it all quiet.

TOM. What are we doin' here, Grace?

GRACE *(overlapping)*. And Miss Wiley says they're gonna close down here—

TOM *(overlapping)*. Grace. Grace!

GRACE. And move across the river. To New York—to open up another factory. Like nothin' ever happened—

TOM. What are we doin' here! I thought the idea was ya'd get some money to settle your debts—get a better doctor—and we'd get on with things.

GRACE. Get on with things.

TOM. You're still wearin' my ring. *(His words yank her out of her tirade.)*

GRACE. Oh, Tommy.

TOM *(taking her hand)*. Grace. There's a house for sale in my brother's neighborhood—Two rooms up, two rooms down, not much, but it's a start. You'll like it. It's already got flowered wallpaper. And best of all—it's only three blocks from the school.

GRACE. The school? What do we need with a school?

TOM. Plan ahead for once. *(A beat.)*

GRACE. Tommy. What do you think is going to happen? After all this is over. D'ya think everything will just go back to the way it was?

TOM. Why wouldn't it? *(A pause.)*

GRACE. I gotta see the surgeon again.

TOM. Uh-huh.

GRACE. I got some fluid. He's gonna drain it.

TOM. Okay.

GRACE. And then, he says. There'll be more.

TOM. So we deal with it when it comes.

GRACE *(overlapping)*. —AND STILL MORE! and then more and still more—why can't you see that? How can you talk about buying houses and getting married when you know there's nothing— *(She stops herself.)*

TOM. Grace. I can't think about that. I just want for us to be together now. I want to come home to you at night. To my wife—my home. I'm too old to be living like this—this, in-between life. I promise, Grace. I'll do whatever it takes to make it easy for you. *(A silence. GRACE takes off her ring and holds it out to him.)*

GRACE. Here.

TOM. Grace. Come on.

GRACE. I shoulda give it back to you a long time ago.

TOM. I don't want it.

GRACE. Tommy. Please. Are ya gonna make me say it?

TOM. You just need to get some rest. That's all. You're not gettin' enough sleep. I'll be back to see you tomorrow—

GRACE. Tommy!

TOM. You get some sleep.

GRACE. Tommy. Tommy! Don't you do this to me. TOMMY!

columbinus

By the United States Theatre Project
Written by Stephen Karam and PJ Paparelli
Dramaturgy by Patricia Hersch
Conceived by PJ Paparelli.

Columbine High School, April, 1999. This script uses police records and other primary source materials to examine the infamous school shootings, their background and their ramifications. Included is this conversation between a teacher and a 911 dispatcher.

DISPATCHER
TEACHER

***

DISPATCHER. Jefferson County 911…

TEACHER. Yes, I'm a teacher at Columbine High School and there is a student here with a gun. He just shot out a window. I believe, um, um.

DISPATCHER. Columbine High School?

TEACHER. I don't know what's in my shoulder. If it was just some glass or what.

DISPATCHER. Has anyone been injured, ma'am?

TEACHER. I am, yes … yes!

DISPATCHER. Okay.

TEACHER. Yes! … and the school is in a panic, and I'm in the library. I've got … students down. *(To students.)* Under the table, kids, heads under the table! Kids are screaming, and the teachers are trying to take control of things. We need police here …

DISPATCHER. Okay, we're getting them there.

TEACHER. Can you please hurry!

DISPATCHER. Who is the student, ma'am?

TEACHER. I do not know who the student is.

DISPATCHER. Okay.

TEACHER. I saw a student outside … I was in the hall … Oh Dear God … Okay, I was on hall duty. I saw a gun and said, "What's going on out there?" And this kid said "Oh, it's probably a video production, probably a joke." *(Talking to student.)* I said, "Well, I don't think that's a good idea," and … I went walking outside … to see what was going on. He turned the gun straight at us and shot and … oh my God, the window went out. And the kid standing there with me, I think he got hit.

DISPATCHER. Okay.

TEACHER. I have something in my shoulder.

DISPATCHER. Okay, we got help on the way, ma'am.

(Large bang.)

TEACHER. Okay ... Oh God!

DISPATCHER. Stay on the line with me *(Large bang.)*

TEACHER. Oh God! Kids, stay down.

DISPATCHER. Do we know where he's at?

TEACHER. I'm sorry.

DISPATCHER. Do we know where he's at?

TEACHER. Okay ... I'm in the library. He's upstairs. He's right outside here.

DISPATCHER. Outside of the hall or outside—

TEACHER. In the hall.

DISPATCHER. Okay.

TEACHER. There are alarms and things going off. Smoke ... *(Yelling:)* My God, smoke is coming into this room.

DISPATCHER. Okay ... I just want you to stay on the line with me. We need to know what's going on.

TEACHER. Okay. I am on the floor.

DISPATCHER. Okay, you've got the kids there?

TEACHER. In the library ... and I've got every student IN THE LIBRARY ON THE FLOOR. *(To students.)* AND YOU GOTTA STAY ON THE FLOOR!

DISPATCHER. Is there any way you can lock the doors?

TEACHER. Um ... smoke is coming in from out there, and ... *(gun fire)* the gun is right outside the library door ... Okay, I don't think I'm going to go out there.

DISPATCHER. Okay, you're at Columbine High School?

TEACHER. I've got three children.

DISPATCHER. Okay we've got it ...

TEACHER. Okay ... I'm ...

DISPATCHER. Yes ...

TEACHER. I'm going to go to the door to shut the door, Okay ... I've got the kids on the floor, um ... I got all the kids in the library on the ...

True Stories Told in Scenes and Monologues | 43

DISPATCHER. We have paramedics, we have fire and police en route … Okay … sir?

TEACHER. Okay.

DISPATCHER. Is there any way you can block the door, so no one can get in?

TEACHER. I … yes … I guess I can try to go, but I mean like he's right outside that door. I'm afraid to go to that door.

DISPATCHER. That's okay.

TEACHER. That's where he is. I don't know. I said, "What … what has that kid got?" He was outside at the time. And … and … and … um. I was on hall duty. *(Explosion.)* Oh God … And he was going, he was like woo, hoo, woo hoo …

DISPATCHER. Mmm-hmm, I know.

TEACHER. … like getting shot off. I said, "What's going on out there?" … said it's a cap gun, probably a video production. You know they do these videos.

DISPATCHER. Right.

TEACHER. That's not, you know, a play gun, a real gun, I was going out there to say, "No" and I went walk— *(Huge gun fire.)* Oh my God, oh my God, that was really close.

Duets: Female

Phillis: A Life of Phillis Wheatley

By Martha Hill Newell

From the moment Phillis Wheatley's poems are made public in the late 1700s, their authenticity is challenged. In this conversation, she expresses every artist's need to have her art appreciated for itself, no matter her background or social standing.

SUSANNAH
PHILLIS

***

SUSANNAH. It is not too late to change your plans, Phillis. Lady Beatrice will understand.

[(PRINCE puts down the trunk and goes out; SUKEY follows.)]

PHILLIS *(as she continues to pack)*. But I would not. Mistress, is it not true that my poems have brought me a certain fame here in Boston?

SUSANNAH. Of course. Sometimes perfect strangers will come up to John and me to inquire about you.

PHILLIS. When they do, what do you tell them?

SUSANNAH. That you write remarkable compositions in verse.

PHILLIS. And what else?

SUSANNAH. That you possess keen intelligence … that you have mastered our language in a few years … that you are highly literate. That I—we—take pride in you!

PHILLIS. And that this is all the more remarkable because I am a *slave*, a native African, belonging to John and Susannah Wheatley?

SUSANNAH. I never call you a slave! I call you …

PHILLIS. What, mistress?

SUSANNAH. I call you a sweet and devoted—companion.

PHILLIS. I want to be called a *poet*!

SUSANNAH. But you are. You have received praise and adulation everywhere!

PHILLIS. Mistress, would I not be deluded if I did not suspect the *reason* for what Reverend Lyon calls the "commotion about Phillis Wheatley"?

SUSANNAH. He is an ignorant man.

PHILLIS. But he is right! The commotion about Phillis Wheatley is about a *slave* girl who is educated. Do you think I am not aware of that?

Mistress, I know I am favored here in this house. You and your family showed me an open door. I walked through that door and far beyond. By myself. And I will keep on going … until my poems are read for themselves. Not because they are written by a slave girl. I want people to read my poems for the *words*. The words first!

SUSANNAH. I see.

PHILLIS. That is why I must go to England. The lady has asked to receive me. I must find out if she and her friends want to receive the slave girl or the poet.

SUSANNAH. Suppose they turn you into a mere plaything?

PHILLIS. I am willing to take the risk.

SUSANNAH. Just to prove a point to stupid people like Lyon?

PHILLIS. He is only a part of it. I have to prove it to myself too.

SUSANNAH. You don't have to prove anything! Phillis, you belong here. This is your home now. Isn't it enough that we love you?

PHILLIS. No … it is not enough.

SUSANNAH. Oh, Phillis. *(Embracing her.)* You must take care of yourself. I've heard that a sea voyage can be very beneficial for weak lungs. But the air can be damp. You have to be careful.

PHILLIS. I will wear the shawl at all times. And I will be *home* soon.

Across the Plains:
The Journey of the Palace Wagon Family
By Sandra Fenichel Asher

In the brutal winter of 1846-1847, a group of emigrants traveling from Illinois to California by wagon train become trapped in the Sierra Nevada mountains by blizzards. Many die of illness and starvation. But even with her husband banished from the group, Margaret Reed keeps herself and her four children alive, including her eldest, Virginia.

MARGARET
VIRGINIA

***

MARGARET. Sit up, Virginia. I've made you some soup. I gathered the beef bones the others had no more use for and boiled them down to a broth. There's no meat left, but there's a bit of flavor still. And marrow. The marrow will give you strength. *(A pause.)* Virginia? *(No answer.)* Virginia, wake up! *(Still no answer; MARGARET slams down bowl, distraught.)* Don't do this to me! Don't you dare … ! *(A pause, then with renewed determination.)* Open your eyes, Virginia! LOOK AT ME!

VIRGINIA *(very weakly)*. I can't, Ma.

MARGARET *(nearly overwhelmed with relief)*. My God!

VIRGINIA. I just want to sleep. I'm … so … tired.

MARGARET. Please, daughter, take a little soup. You've got to eat—

VIRGINIA. It makes no difference …

MARGARET. *We must stay alive!*

VIRGINIA. Why?

MARGARET. Because your sister and brothers depend on us—

VIRGINIA. Maybe they shouldn't—

MARGARET. But they DO! You *will* sit up, daughter, and you *will* eat. You *will* go on living, as I do, no matter how tired you are. *That is your duty!* You will be here to greet your father with the rest of us when he returns.

VIRGINIA. *If* he returns! Oh, why did you listen to him, Ma? Why did you let him bring us to this?

MARGARET. *Don't* … torment me with those questions. Do you think I haven't asked them of myself often enough?

VIRGINIA. And your answer?

MARGARET. There is none. None that matters now.

VIRGINIA. I thought he was a hero.

MARGARET. He may prove to be one—

VIRGINIA. Do you believe that?

MARGARET. I believe—we must do the best we can. *(A pause, then she smiles.)* And as long as you're sitting up, try the soup. *(VIRGINIA laughs weakly. With MARGARET's help, she begins to eat.)* There! That's better, isn't it? *(VIRGINIA nods, takes another sip.)* Virginia, your father needs us … to forgive him.

VIRGINIA. I'm not sure I can.

A Midnight Cry:
The Underground Railroad To Freedom

By James DeVita
Musical selections and arrangements by Josh Schmidt
Additional selections and arrangements by Sheri Williams Panell

Lida Anderson has been whipped for protesting the sale of her little sister. Her behavior has now marked her for continual mistreatment. She and her mother must consider the necessity for escape—and its dangers.

LIDA
MAMA

***

LIDA. No one ever be the same after they been whipped. It scar your soul. It was near a month 'fore I could use my arms again. When I get back to work Mr. Bullard he waitin' for me. I can't do nuthin' right. He beat me he don't like the way the sun look that day. He wake up lookin' to hurt me. *(MAMA and LIDA billow the same sheets above their heads and let them fall before them, transforming the scene to the two of them kneeling side by side doing wash. Real time. Scrubbing clothes.)* What you know about these free states, Mama?

MAMA. Hush up, child. Don't be askin' such questions.

LIDA. I gonna keep askin' till I finds out, Mama, might as well come from you.

MAMA. You get caught talkin' such things they gonna whip you again, maybe sell you off.

LIDA. Mama, they don't need no reason to sell a body off. Look what happened to baby Keeley. And Mr. Bullard gonna kill me one way o' da other he have his way. I'd rather get kilt tryin' to be free than fo' scrubbin' his filthy clothes the wrong way. Now, you tell me or I'ze gonna run off and find out ma'self. Is there really places where all people be free?

MAMA *(beat)*. Yes.

LIDA. There is!? Then why you 'n Papa never try to get there?

MAMA. Shh! What you mean never try? Where yo' sense, girl? I ha' chillun I responsible fo', and yo' daddy be near to crippled fo' half his life from tryin' to be free. Tha's right, 'fore any one even knowed o' these free states he run off. Say he gonna be free and live in da woods like da Indians, come back and steal us free once he know the way. He make it to one o' these free states everyone talkin' about, but they find him dere and drag him back anyway. They close to kill him they beat 'im so bad. Broke dat po' man's body like they snappin' twigs. So you watch yo' tone with me.

LIDA. I didn't know, Mama.

MAMA. Yeah, they's lots you don't know. More than you ever needs to be burdened with. *(Beat.)* But yo' right. It ain't safe fo' you here no more. I seen that look in Bullard's eyes. Uncle Eli know about these things. We talk to Uncle Eli.

Sounds of Silents (The Essanay Years)

By Paul Peditto

Destined for stardom but in no way prepared for it, Gloria Swanson arrives at Essanay Studios young, naïve, and full of attitude. Experienced silent film actress Beverly Bayne is assigned the daunting task of training her.

BEVERLY BAYNE
GLORIA SWANSON

***

BAYNE. Technique! Motion picture acting is technique. We begin with the ABCs and extend to higher difficulty. Begin anew.

SWANSON. I don't understand.

BAYNE. Understand, Miss Swanson?

SWANSON. I already know how to sit and walk!

BAYNE. Lines are drawn on the floor. You must hit your mark. If you miss, you go out of frame, the shot is ruined. You must practice the basics: How to stand, how to walk across a room, how to sit. You must unlearn everything and relearn it for the camera. If you want to see your name in the electric lights of the Rialto. *(BAYNE turns and SWANSON sticks her tongue out at her.)* Great work awaits the girl who can screen beautifully and think beautifully. The need is for a heart and brain to go with the pretty face.

SWANSON *(mumbling)*. Nonsense.

BAYNE. Pardon me?

SWANSON. All this strutting and prancing … it seems, well … stupid.

BAYNE. Stop. *(SWANSON stops.)* Stupid, is it?

SWANSON. I think so.

BAYNE. Upstage demeanor from a sixteen-year-old. *(Furious.)* We all kick in here and do what needs to be done. We're friends and equals and I'll do my part—but not much more, by God.

SWANSON. I didn't mean to speak out.

BAYNE. Of course you didn't. You were just overcome by self-fascination. *(Closer.)* Do you know how lucky you are? How many girls would kill to be in your shoes? Mr. Spoor chose you! He could have thrown you out and gotten any of a dozen others to take your place!

SWANSON. Well, why didn't he then!?

BAYNE. Maybe he should have! *(BAYNE/SWANSON back off.)* Maybe … he liked your nerve.

SWANSON. Nerve?

BAYNE. One rarely meets an ingenue with beauty and brains.

SWANSON. I've no more brains than a snail. I don't even know what I'm doing here.

BAYNE. You've enough brains to see you don't know anything about acting, but enough humility to learn.

SWANSON. I wanted to be an actress so I could live in a beautiful home, feeding upon hothouse dainties served on monogrammed china.

BAYNE. Monogrammed china?

SWANSON. Like in the movie magazines.

BAYNE. You say the damnedest things! My meals are eaten in basements, in freezing autos, cold and tired, mouthing a lunch of some uncertain sandwich with a glass of stale milk.

SWANSON. But the money you make—

BAYNE. Young lady, I am not in the millionaire class! Watching you stand up and sit down and prance around for the sport of it! *(Both break into smiles.)* Oh, come along!

The Face of Emmett Till

By Mamie Till-Mobley and David Barr III

After her son Emmett's abduction and murder in August, 1955, Mamie Till-Mobley does all she can to bring those responsible to justice, including public appearances that keep the case in the public eye. Death threats and obscene letters and phone calls follow. Her mother falls victim to a cruel attempt to stop her activities.

ALMA
MAMIE

***

ALMA. Yes? *(Beat.)* Yes. This is the Spearman residence. *(Beat.)* What? *(Long pause. ALMA bursts into tears of joy. She is almost debilitated with jubilation.)* What?!! You what?!!!! Praise Him!!!! Praise God!!!!!

MAMIE *(confused and suspicious)*. Mama?

ALMA *(ignoring MAMIE. Barely able to hold the telephone)*. Bless you, sir!!! God bless you!!!!

MAMIE *(more pointed.)* Who *is* that, Mama?

ALMA *(lost in her own euphoria)*. When can I … I mean … when can *we* see him?!

MAMIE. Mama, I don't think you should …

ALMA. No … no, you're right. That won't be necessary. We'll just wait to hear from you!!!! *Bless you, sir!!! Bless you!!!* You've made us all … *so happy!!!!* (ALMA hangs up.)

MAMIE. Mama, what is it?

ALMA *(grabbing MAMIE. Falling to her knees with joy. Almost in a state of delirium)*. They found him, Mamie!!!! They've found Emmett!!!! And he's alive!!! Emmett…is alive!!!!

MAMIE *(confused. Getting upset)*. What? What are you talking about? Who was that?

ALMA. I don't know. Some … man. He said that he was a police officer. And that he had been working with the FBI on Emmett's case. But it doesn't matter who he is!!! Nothing else matters right now. They've found Emmett!!!! *And he's alive!!!! He's comin' back to us!!!*

MAMIE *(slowing down. Suspiciously)*. What else did this man say?

ALMA *(panting. Out of breath with happiness)*. He said … that *everything* … this whole incident … was just a terrible mix-up and that Emmett has been alive all this time! He said … he said that there wasn't any more need for you to keep talkin' to the newspapers. There ain't no need for any kind of police investigation … or even for you to go to Mississippi. *Because he's coming home! (Half-beat.)* The man also said … that you don't have to fly around the country anymore makin' all those speeches for the NAACP.

MAMIE *(pause. Fighting back emotion).* Mama, please … *don't do this.*

ALMA *(about to lose it. Delirium).* I've got to call Henry!!!!

MAMIE. Just stop for a minute … and listen to what you're saying.

ALMA. I've got to let him know that …

MAMIE. Mama … please … stop! *(Beat.)* Did this man tell you why he's waited all of this time to call us? Or why he's kept silent even after the sheriff in Money arrested the two white men who took Emmett from the house? Did he give you a reason why he let the district attorney set a trial date before calling us? *(Tears welling in her eyes.)* Did this man even let you speak with my Emmett?

ALMA *(long pause. Reality sets in. Realizing that phone call was nothing but a cruel hoax. She breaks down).* No. No! Emmett *is* alive. He's coming back to us. Why can't you just accept that?

MAMIE. Emmett is gone. He's gone, Mama.

ALMA. *But …* that man on the telephone said …

MAMIE. No.

ALMA *(beat. Slow implosion).* Oh God!!!! *(Half-beat.)* God. *(Beat. MAMIE embraces her, crestfallen.)* Why?

MAMIE. I'm here, Mama. I'm here. We've just got to hold on … until we find the answers. *(Lights slowly fade and end scene.)*

Duets: Male

Free Man of Color

By Charles Smith

Upon successfully graduating from Ohio University in 1828, John Newton Templeton is offered the governorship of Liberia, a colony designated to become a sovereign nation populated by freed American slaves. He and his mentor, Reverend Robert Wilson, disagree on the benevolence of this plan.

WILSON
JOHN

***

WILSON. Somebody spotted some Indians not far from here. That's the reason for the pistol.

JOHN. Indians?

WILSON. Every now and then you come across a couple of stragglers. That's what these probably are. Stragglers living in the caves in the out-lying regions. Nothing to worry about. The government's going to send out some riders to track them down. They'll find them, relocate them. Send them to live with the rest of their people.

JOHN. If there's nothing to worry about, why do you need a pistol?

WILSON. You never can be too safe. Besides, you're going to need to know how to fire a pistol once you get to Liberia. Now, check to make sure that the barrel is clear. Once you're sure that the barrel is clear, you add your powder charge.

JOHN. What do I do about the people who are already there?

WILSON. Already where? What people?

JOHN. In Liberia. When I get there, what do I do about the people already there?

WILSON. It's a wilderness, John. There are no people there.

JOHN. Natives. What do I do about the natives?

WILSON. That's up to you. You offer them the word and if they refuse that word … *(Beat.)*

JOHN. If they refuse?

WILSON. I suggest that you give them the option of determining their own fate. If they refuse the word then one option would be to relocate them. Not you, personally, of course. You'll have men to do that for you. Now check your barrel. Make sure it's clear.

JOHN. Where does it stop?

WILSON. Where does what stop?

JOHN. I relocate the people who are there, they relocate someone else. Where does it stop?

WILSON. Relocation is only an option, John. They don't have to be relocated. They can accept the gift of civilization.

JOHN. I'm not quite sure it's a gift.

WILSON. What're you talking about?

JOHN. We seem to be caught in this vicious circle. The English came to Ireland, the Irish came to America, now you're sending me to Liberia. Where do the Liberians go?

WILSON. I'm sure you'll be able to find a place for them.

JOHN. The way Andrew Jackson found a place for the Shawnee?

WILSON. Are you trying to be insolent?

JOHN. I don't think I'm the right man for this.

WILSON. 'Course you are, John.

JOHN. I feel like I'm giving up without even trying. You said your father fought against the English. But he fought. He didn't give up when somebody asked him to move. He fought, he struggled, he tried to keep his home before striking out to find a new home. And even then, he didn't abandon that fight until after it became clear that he couldn't win that fight. Here I am, I haven't even tried.

WILSON. Tried what?

JOHN. Tried to make this my home. I've given up without even trying.

WILSON. But this is not your home, John. Your home is in Africa.

JOHN. My home is here in the United States.

WILSON. But your people are from Africa.

JOHN. And your people are from Ireland but I don't see you getting on a boat to go back. My family has been in this country for six generations. Five generations longer than your family. My father cut and fitted by hand every single piece of wood in the main library of the White House. But yet, you tell me that I'm the one who has to go? No, I'm sorry, but I can't do it, I won't do it. Not without first trying to make this my home.

Keeping Mr. Lincoln

By Sandra Fenichel Asher

The Civil War rages on and its toll hangs heavy on the nation. Scores of people arrive at the White House each day, lining up to speak to President Abraham Lincoln and begging favors of all kinds. The plight of John Bullock, a young Southerner, touches him deeply.

BULLOCK
LINCOLN

***

BULLOCK *(to audience)*. I returned to the White House at four and saw the president standing upon the west end of the front portico. I discovered that he was negotiating for the purchase of a horse suitable for one of his sons. An orderly was riding a stylish-looking animal up and down a driveway.

LINCOLN THREE *(motions BULLOCK closer [as MRS. LINCOLN exits])*. You are a Kentuckian and ought to know something about horses. Tell me, what do you think that one is worth? *(He points offstage, toward "horse.")*

BULLOCK. He appears to be a fairly good saddle horse, sir. Perhaps one hundred and fifty dollars.

LINCOLN THREE. Just what I said! But that fellow wants two hundred. I'll stand by my offer. *(Guides BULLOCK into office, motions him to a chair; takes one facing him.)* Now, what can I do for you?

BULLOCK. Mr. President, I have come to ask you to parole my brother from Johnson's Island. Lieutenant W.R. Bullock. He is extremely ill and I want you to release him so that he may be brought home to die.

LINCOLN THREE. Will your brother take the oath?

BULLOCK. The oath, sir?

LINCOLN THREE. Of allegiance. To the Union.

BULLOCK. No, sir. He will die in prison if that is the only alternative.

LINCOLN THREE. Then I can not parole him. It is impossible unless he will take the oath.

BULLOCK. Sir, my brother cannot live long in his present condition, and it would be a great comfort to our invalid mother to have him brought home so that he can be tenderly nursed until he dies.

LINCOLN THREE. My son, I should like to grant your request, but I cannot do it. *(Stands and turns away, torn by his dilemma.)* You don't know what pressure is brought to bear upon me in such matters.

BULLOCK *(turns away, disheartened; then, with nothing left to lose—).* Mr. Lincoln, you are the only person in the country that can do absolutely as you please in such matters. You can release him if you desire to do so, no matter what people think. *(LINCOLN THREE considers BULLOCK's challenge. To audience—)* The president sank into a state of deep meditation. He had that faraway look in his eyes so often spoken of by those who knew him during those awful years of blood and carnage, when his great soul was wrung with the anguish of a nation at war with itself. *(Beat.)* I watched him … and waited … and clung to his words, "We must not be enemies."

(LINCOLN THREE turns "suddenly, without warning, his whole being alert, his eyes clear and strong." He walks over to table, writes quickly on a visiting card and holds it out to Bullock who takes it.)

BULLOCK *(reading).* "Allow Lieutenant W.R. Bullock to be paroled and go to his parents in Baltimore. A. Lincoln."

LINCOLN THREE. That'll fetch him.

BULLOCK. Thank you, sir!

The Radiance of a Thousand Suns: The Hiroshima Project

By Anne V. McGravie, Dwight Okita, Nicholas A. Patricca and David Zak
Music by Chuck Larkin

The invitation to work on a secret project with brilliant physicist J. Robert Oppenheimer is an irresistible siren call to two Princeton graduate students. The results of their work will change the world and alter the course of their own lives.

FEYNMAN
PHYSICIST

***

PHYSICIST. In the summer of 1943, when I was a grad student at Princeton getting ready to take my qualifying exams, Richard Feynman, a fellow student and the most brilliant and eccentric person I had ever met, cornered me in the physics library john.

FEYNMAN. Hurry up. We're going on a trip.

PHYSICIST. I'm not going anywhere.

FEYNMAN. I already packed your bag.

PHYSICIST. You're so thoughtful.

FEYNMAN. And don't worry about money.

PHYSICIST. I'm not worried about money. I'm worried about my exams. I'm not like you. I need to study.

FEYNMAN. Forget exams. This trip is important.

PHYSICIST. No exams. No degree. No degree. No marriage. Rachel is already counting the weeks till we can set a date.

FEYNMAN. I guess I made a mistake. I thought you were a physicist.

PHYSICIST. What the hell is that supposed to mean?

FEYNMAN. It means you're supposed to zip the zipper on your pants. Wash your hands. And go with me without asking stupid questions.

PHYSICIST. Go where?

FEYNMAN. I can't tell you.

PHYSICIST. Why not?

FEYNMAN. Because it's possibly the most important scientific project in human history and when they said they wanted me to work on it with the best scientists in the whole world, I said I couldn't possibly do it without the knowledge and skill of my friend. Besides, Oppenheimer wants you.

PHYSICIST. Oppenheimer wants me?!

[AGENT. OK, Feynman, time to go. Is he coming or not?]

FEYNMAN *(to AGENT)*. He's coming. I said he'd come and he's coming. *(To PHYSICIST.)* He works for the government: top secret, hush hush, and all that baloney. I told him you'd come. I told him: I know a physicist when I meet one. I'm never wrong about that.

PHYSICIST *(to AUDIENCE)*. Feynman and I drove all the way to Los Alamos. My life was never the same again.

Jackie & Me

By Steven Dietz
Adapted from the book by Dan Gutman

Baseball executive Branch Rickey knows the challenges of breaking the sport's color barrier, and he knows what's needed to meet those challenges—extraordinary athletic talent plus unshakable personal character and emotional strength. In 1947, he finds all of that and more in one man—Jackie Robinson.

BRANCH RICKEY
JACKIE

***

BRANCH RICKEY *(finally)*. You know why you're here?

JACKIE. Yes, sir. A fellow told me to meet with you. Said you were gonna start up a Negro League team here in Brooklyn. The Brown Dodgers.

BRANCH RICKEY. Yes, that was my plan. Till I had a new thought. A bigger thought.

(BRANCH RICKEY and JACKIE continue to stare at each other across the room.)

BRANCH RICKEY *(cont'd)*. I've been talking to lot of people, Jack. People out West, in California, who knew you in school. They say at UCLA you lettered in four sports in one year.

JACKIE. That's true.

BRANCH RICKEY. And no one had ever done that. Only you.

JACKIE. Yes, sir.

BRANCH RICKEY. And baseball was your best sport?

JACKIE. No, sir. It was my worst.

BRANCH RICKEY. You were even better at football and basketball and track?

JACKIE. Yes, sir.

(Beat.)

BRANCH RICKEY *(quickly)*. I could beat you at tennis.

JACKIE *(just as quick)*. No sir, you could not.

BRANCH RICKEY. Bowling.

JACKIE. No.

BRANCH RICKEY. Horseshoes, Checkers, Ping-Pong.

JACKIE. No, no and no.

BRANCH RICKEY. You don't lose, is that it?

JACKIE. *Not happily, no.*

BRANCH RICKEY. *Neither do I, Jack. (Beat.)* But I'm talking about doing something that's never been done.

JACKIE. You're not starting up a team here in Brooklyn, are you, Mr. Rickey?

BRANCH RICKEY. No, Jack, I've already got a team. They're called the Dodgers. And I want you to play for 'em.

[JOEY (to audience). Finally! Now all that had to happen was for Jackie Robinson to say yes!

(JOEY turns expectantly to JACKIE. JACKIE is silent.)

JOEY *(cont'd, exasperated).* But he didn't say anything!

(The PHONE RINGS and JOEY immediately answers it.)

JOEY *(cont'd).* I SAID HOLD MY CALLS—*we're tryin' to make some history here!*

(JOEY hangs up the phone, hard, as BRANCH RICKEY shoots him a look. JOEY returns to where he was watching.)]

BRANCH RICKEY *(to JACKIE).* You're a polite young man. Credit to your mother. She taught you good manners.

JACKIE. Yes, sir, she did.

BRANCH RICKEY. So, where'd you get that temper? Word is you're a hothead, Robinson. You were a hothead in the military and you're the same way on the field. You've got a mean streak in you, an angry streak—is that true?

JACKIE. I suppose you could—

BRANCH RICKEY *(sharply).* I suppose you could ANSWER THE QUESTION.

(A hard, sharp look from JACKIE to BRANCH RICKEY.)

JACKIE *(icily).* I have a temper, yes.

BRANCH RICKEY. Good. You're gonna need it. And you're gonna need to know *how to use it.* See, I know you can hit and run and throw, but that's not gonna be enough.

(BRANCH RICKEY stands and approaches JACKIE, building in intensity.)

BRANCH RICKEY *(cont'd).* What'll you do, Jack? When all your teammates go to a restaurant and you're not allowed to eat there? When you have to stay in a separate hotel, ride on a separate bus, walk in the back door rather than the front?!

JACKIE. I'll do what it takes, Mr. Rickey.

BRANCH RICKEY. Well, I hope you know what it "takes" when those voices start sayin', "Hey Nappy Head, get your butt to the back of the line."

JACKIE *(trying to stay cool).* Mr. Rickey—

BRANCH RICKEY. "Where'd you steal that suit—off the back of a white man?"

JACKIE. Please, sir—

BRANCH RICKEY. "Why don't you go back to the cotton fields where you belong? Baseball's a white man's game—"

JACKIE. Listen now—

BRANCH RICKEY *(overlapping).* "And uppity coons like you are fit for nothin' but shining our shoes, ain't that right?!"

(JACKIE's fists are now clenched at his side, rage in his eyes, as BRANCH RICKEY makes a fist, like he's about to punch JACKIE.)

BRANCH RICKEY *(cont'd).* I said, "AIN'T THAT RIGHT, BOY??!!"

(A frozen moment: BRANCH RICKEY's fist is ready to strike. JACKIE is staring fiercely into BRANCH RICKEY's eyes.)

BRANCH RICKEY *(cont'd, quietly, a hard whisper).* What will you do, Jack, when you hear all that?

JACKIE. You want a man who's *afraid to fight back?*

BRANCH RICKEY. No. *I want a man with enough courage NOT TO.* *(Beat.)* A man who knows how to use his temper. I want him to put his temper into *the game.* If you lash out at ANYONE—even ONCE—it's over. You'd have to promise me. You'd have to learn to turn to the other cheek. *(Beat.)* Can you do that, Jack?

(Silence.)

[JOEY (whispers to audience). And after a very long silence, Jackie Robinson said ...]

JACKIE. Yes, sir.

(BRANCH RICKEY extends his hand and JACKIE, after staring at it for a moment, shakes his hand.)

[JOEY (quietly). Yes!]

BRANCH RICKEY. I've got some papers for you to sign.

Stand and Deliver

Based on the screenplay by Ramón Menéndez and Tom Musca
Adapted for the stage by Robert Bella

East Los Angeles, 1987. Gangs, drugs and drop-outs are daunting enough challenges to Jaime Escalante's plan to take his inner-city math students to new academic heights. But well-meaning parents also stand in his way.

ESCALANTE
DELGADO

***

ESCALANTE *(smiling)*. Mr. Delgado. How are you?

DELGADO. **Mucho gusto.**

ESCALANTE. To what do I owe this pleasure?

[ANA. I can't stay in your class.

ESCALANTE. Why not?

ANA. My—]

DELGADO. Anita … Señior Escalante, I have a family restaurant. Already she spends too much time studying. Now, with the extra work from your class, **imposible** … So. Señior Molina said we need your signature—

ESCALANTE. No way. I won't sign. Ana should stay in this class. She's top kid.

DELGADO. The restaurant needs her.

ESCALANTE. You should hire another waitress. Ana can be the first one in your family to graduate from high school. Go to college.

DELGADO. I thank you for your concern, Mr. Escalante. But, her mother works there, her sisters, her brothers. This is a family business. She has responsibilities.

ESCALANTE. What about responsibility to her future? She could help the family more by getting an education.

DELGADO. Ahhh, probably get married. She wouldn't finish college.

[ANA. Papa.

DELGADO. Ana! **Espera afuera.** *(ANA is close to tears as she leaves the classroom. She waits in the hall as the MEN resume the debate.)]*

ESCALANTE. She talks about going to medical school.

DELGADO. No. I don't think so.

ESCALANTE. She should make her own choices.

DELGADO. **Un momento! Yo soy el padre de la niña, no usted!**

ESCALANTE. She'll just get fat and stupid. She'll waste her life away in your restaurant. She's top kid!

DELGADO. I started washing dishes for a nickel an hour. Now, I own that restaurant. Did I waste my life?!

ESCALANTE. I washed dishes too, when I first came to this country. But that—

DELGADO. Good! Strap on an apron. Come by and give us a hand.

ESCALANTE *(overlapping)*. She could go to college, come back and teach you how to run the place.

DELGADO. Professor, I know how to run my own family! Now, please, the signature. *(Reluctantly, ESCALANTE signs the paper.)*

ESCALANTE. Mr. Delgado, you've obviously done well for your family. If you believe yourself to be a good father, you must believe you raised your daughter to make the right decisions on her own … Please sir, I just want what's best for Ana.

DELGADO. So do I, Mr. Escalante. So do I.

Trios

The Indian Captive

Developed from history by Charlotte B. Chorpenning

Eight months after Eleanor Lytell's abduction—and loving adoption—by Seneca Indians in 1779, her mother's long and persistent search finally brings her as close as possible to a reunion. Having learned the Seneca language, Mrs. Lytell speaks to two Seneca children.

MRS. LYTELL
REDBILL
SHINING LEAVES

***

MRS. LYTELL. If you are Seneca children, you will understand what I say.

(REDBILL and SHINING LEAVES exchange glances, excited and a little frightened. [CORNPLANTER enters silently, upstage, and stands watching them, unseen by any of them.])

MRS. LYTELL *(cont'd)*. Do not be afraid. I am a friend of the Senecas. I have learned to speak their tongue that I may talk to them as brothers. *(The children make no response. She comes a little closer.)* Speak to me, Seneca boy. I wait for the sound of your voice.

REDBILL. I have no word to speak to you.

MRS. LYTELL *(touching SHINING LEAVES)*. Will you speak a word of welcome to me, Seneca maid? I had a daughter who has seen as many summers as you. Eight moons ago, I came to my lodge and found it empty as a nest the birds have left last summer. My daughter had been taken away. I have walked night and day asking at every Seneca village: Do my brothers know of any white captive? Many have said to me, "We have heard of a white girl who dwells in Cornplanter's village." I have come here, searching for news of her.

REDBILL. We have no news to give you.

MRS. LYTELL. Have you never heard anyone speak of a captive, in the village yonder?

REDBILL. The Old Queen says to us: Talk flies about the campfire like the wind that blows this way and that. Pay no heed to it.

MRS. LYTELL. Who are you? Your dress is Seneca. Do you live in Cornplanter's village?

REDBILL. My name is Redbill.

MRS. LYTELL *(touching SHINING LEAVES)*. And this maid?

SHINING LEAVES. My name is Shining Leaves.

MRS. LYTELL. What pretty names. And what are you called, busy one who will not look up from her work?

[(ELEANOR bends her head still lower, keeping on with her work. CORNPLANTER is deeply interested.)]

MRS. LYTELL *(cont'd)*. Won't you tell me your name?

REDBILL. Her name is Ship-under-full-sail. She won't tell it, because she does not like white people.

[(ELEANOR is disturbed by this, but swallows it without a sign, except the face.)]

MRS. LYTELL. Why not? *(Eagerly.)* Did you ever know a white child? Won't you tell me, Ship-under-full-sail?

[(ELEANOR starts to gather up her work.)]

REDBILL. You are making her go away.

MRS. LYTELL. Never mind, busy maid. I'll not talk to you. What pretty things you're making, Shining Leaves.

SHINING LEAVES. I'm making the sky blue water on mine. Ship-under-full-sail is making the little day-time moon. See?

MRS. LYTELL *(picking it up)*. The little day-time moon. Ah! Do you suppose my daughter has learned to make such pretty things as this?

SHINING LEAVES *(in a burst of enthusiasm)*. She can make the finest bead work and quill work of us all! *(Suddenly covers her mouth with her hand.)*

MRS. LYTELL. What?! What did you say?!

REDBILL *(to SHINING LEAVES, angrily)*. You make a trail with your words, like the mole who lifts his burrow plain in the earth for the hunter to see!

MRS. LYTELL. You know her! You have seen her! Take me to her! I will give you many gifts if you will take me to her.

REDBILL. That is not for us to do.

MRS. LYTELL. I will ask your chief. At last I have found her! Is she well? Is she strong?

SHINING LEAVES. She beats all of us in the races for the girls.

MRS. LYTELL. Are they kind to her?

REDBILL. She is a sister to Cornplanter, the chief, and a daughter to the Old Queen, his mother. The best pieces in the pot of meat Cornplanter fishes out to give her.

SHINING LEAVES. She has the finest garments in the village. The Old Queen makes them herself.

MRS. LYTELL. Is she happy? Does she grieve for her home? Does she long for her mother?

REDBILL. When she came, she grieved much. She went often alone and let her tears fall in secret. She thought we did not know, but we followed her like hunters on the trail, and saw.

[(This is the first time ELEANOR has heard this.)]

SHINING LEAVES. But now she does not do that. She doesn't want to go away.

MRS. LYTELL. She would want to go with me!

REDBILL. You speak foolish words. She is among the Senecas like our sister the birch-tree that gave us this bark, whose roots are in our earth and will not let her be moved.

[(CORNPLANTER is very delighted with this. ELEANOR moves uneasily, but is quiet again.)]

MRS. LYTELL. She cannot have forgotten her brother. She cannot have forgotten her mother so soon. We have thought of her day and night. We knew she was waiting for me to come.

REDBILL. You have listened to bad birds. She does not wish you to come.

MRS. LYTELL *(to herself)*. Oh—if that were true—

Freedom Is My Middle Name

By Lee Hunkins

Mary Eliza Mahoney works at the New England Hospital for Women and Children in Roxbury, Massachusetts, and dreams of becoming a nurse. But she is black, and, in 1878, this is truly an impossible dream. That's not going to stop her.

SARAH
MARY
DR. ZAK

***

SARAH. What time did you get to bed?

MARY. Around two.

SARAH. Your body needs more than four hours sleep.

MARY. I start reading and the next thing I know it's morning. Sarah, there's so much I want to learn.

SARAH. Why don't you get rid of those silly ideas? You ought to take your head out of those books, and start thinkin' about marriage.

MARY. There's time for that.

SARAH. Mary, you're thirty-three years old. Always talkin' about nursin' and it don't make sense!

MARY. It's what I want!

SARAH. Stop dreamin' and make do with what you got!

MARY. Why should I?

SARAH. 'Cause we ain't supposed to be nurses and doctors!

   (DR. ZAK enters and goes to her office.)

MARY. We're just as good as anybody else.

SARAH. Some jobs are meant for white people, and some for colored.

MARY. I wasn't born with a mop in my hand!

SARAH. Well, excuse me, Miss Mahoney! I guess scrubbin' and cleanin' are beneath you.

MARY. I'm not ashamed of being a servant, I just want somethin' more. But you're right, it's time I stopped being a dreamer!

   (MARY walks in the direction of Dr. Zak's office.)

SARAH *(to MARY)*. Where are you going?

MARY. To see Dr. Zak!

SARAH *(calling after her)*. Woman, are you crazy?

(As MARY knocks on Dr. Zak's door and enters, SARAH picks up the bucket and exits.)

DR. ZAK. Good morning, Mary.

MARY. Morning, Dr. Zak. I'm sorry to barge in like this, but can I talk to you for a minute?

DR. ZAK *(motioning MARY to a chair)*. Of course.

MARY. I've been working here fifteen years. I cook, clean, scrub, do whatever's asked of me.

DR. ZAK. Your record is outstanding.

MARY *(hesitantly)*. That's good because … well … I want to apply for the nurse's training program.

DR. ZAK. You what?

MARY *(determined)*. I want to be a nurse.

DR. ZAK. You realize it's sixteen months of hard training?

MARY. Yes.

DR. ZAK. It requires physical strength, too.

MARY. I can lift patients, move beds. I'm stronger than I look.

DR. ZAK. I must be honest with you. We've never had a Negro apply for nurse's training.

MARY. Then I'll be the first.

DR. ZAK *(angrily)*. What put this nonsense in your head? My advice to you is to forget the whole thing! *(She turns away from MARY.)*

MARY. You told a graduating class that your father didn't want you to be a doctor. He sent you to school to be a mid-wife, but you stood up to him and all the others who tried to discourage you.

DR. ZAK *(turning to MARY)*. How did you hear my speech?

MARY. I was cleanin' the hall outside the auditorium. I opened the door … just a little. You said that women have to fight for what they believe in.

DR. ZAK. Yes, but my situation was ...

MARY *(cutting her off)*. Dr. Zak. I can't forget about it. I've had this feeling for such a long time. In my heart I believe … I know I've got to be a nurse.

(Taken aback by MARY's request, DR. ZAK doesn't speak for a few seconds.)

74 | American Heartbeat

DR. ZAK. It would have to be approved by the Board of Directors.

MARY. May I apply?

(DR. ZAK stares at her. MARY doesn't flinch.

SARAH enters, walks down the corridor to outside the hospital, and sits on the bench. DR. ZAK looks through a folder filled with papers. She pulls out an application and gives it to MARY.)

MARY. Thank you. *(MARY walks towards the door.)*

DR. ZAK. Don't get your hopes up. It's not going to be easy.

MARY. I didn't think it would be. *(MARY exits. Once outside the office, she clutches the paper to her chest and twirls around excitedly. She rushes down the corridor, exits the hospital and crosses to SARAH.)* I did it! *(Handing SARAH the application.)* I'm applying for nurse's training! *(SARAH glances at the paper and gives it back.)* Well, say something.

SARAH. What do you want me to say?

MARY. You could wish me luck.

SARAH. You're gonna need more than luck. Mary, they don't want colored women trainin' to be nurses. Cookin' and cleanin' is one thing, but they ain't gonna put you in charge of no white folks!

MARY *(walking to the lounge area)*. I have to fill this out.

SARAH. I want to be happy for you, but I can't. I think you're makin' a big mistake.

The Remeberer

By Steven Dietz
Based on the unpublished memoir As My Sun Now Sets
by Joyce Simmons Cheeka, as told to Werdna Phillips Finley

Though she's been forced to attend a government-run boarding school where she's expected to deny her heritage, Squaxin Indian Joyce Simmons Cheeka is still the chosen "rememberer," charged with preserving the history and culture of her people. Late at night, in secret, she and her fellow students find ways to do just that.

GIRL ONE
JOYCE
GIRL TWO

***

GIRL ONE. What kind of quilt will it be?

JOYCE. A salmon quilt.

GIRL TWO. Where'd you get the cloth?

JOYCE. Where'd you get that knife?

GIRL TWO *(smiles)*. Secret.

JOYCE *(smiles)*. Secret. *(They shake hands.)*

GIRL ONE. I'm hungry.

GIRL TWO. Potatoes, stewed in fish oil.

GIRL ONE *(nods)*. And berries for dessert.

JOYCE. And Emily Sam's "ashes" bread. *(They make hungry moans and groans, playfully. Except for GIRL ONE, who begins to cry, quietly.)*

GIRL ONE. I want to go home. *(The OTHER GIRLS look at her.)*

GIRL TWO. It's all right, Sarah. *(She holds GIRL ONE. Then, she looks up at JOYCE.)* Joyce … tell her a story.

(JOYCE begins to tell a story. As the story progresses, the GIRLS lift a sheet off the bed and drape it up behind the candles. They then use the props in the scene [brush, knife, fabric, bracelet, piece of cedar, etc.] to "act out" a tiny <u>shadow play</u> in the candlelight.)

JOYCE. A long time ago, before the time of the Great Flood, there were two brothers who lived with their grandparents.

One was very dark.

The other was very white.

They fought all the time.

This made their grandparents very angry.

One day, their grandparents said to them:

GIRL TWO. "Now that you have grown into young men, it is time for you to leave."

JOYCE. To the dark brother, they said: "You must go toward where the sun sets and grow with the land. Make a good life. Be useful." Then, to the white brother, they said:

GIRL ONE. "You must go toward where the sun rises. Far from your dark brother. Make your life there."

JOYCE. Then, to both brothers they said:

GIRL TWO. "Because of your fighting, you will never in your lifetime come together again."

JOYCE. "But, someday, many years from now, your <u>children</u>—"

GIRL ONE. "And your <u>children's children</u>—"

GIRL TWO. "May find a way to come together."

JOYCE. "And, on that day, and not before … "

(JOYCE looks at GIRL ONE, who has wiped away her tears.)

GIRL ONE. "They may live together in peace."

JOYCE *(nods)*. "The peace which you never found."

Radium Girls
By D.W. Gregory

Struggling with a mysterious disease that has already killed some of her co-workers, Grace Fryer is urged by many, including factory representative Edward Markley and her own mother, to agree to the settlement offered by her company.

MARKLEY
GRACE
MRS. FRYER

***

MARKLEY. Miss Fryer. Edward Markley. *(He holds out his hand to shake. GRACE doesn't take it. GRACE looks at him, folds her letter away.)*

GRACE. Ma said you brought papers.

MARKLEY. Yes. The terms spelled out as we explained in our letter. Fifteen hundred dollars to you—I've got a check right here. All we need is your signature. *(He gives her the papers. She flips through them.)* It's in triplicate. *(She tries to read, but can't focus.)*

MRS. FRYER. Grace. Mr. Markley is a very busy man.

MARKLEY. Oh, no. Please. Take your time. Look it over carefully. If you prefer, I can leave it and come back tomorrow.

MRS. FRYER. No, no. We'll do this now.

GRACE *(swallows hard)*. What's "hold harmless"?

MARKLEY. You agree to hold the company harmless from any further action.

GRACE. No more law suits.

MARKLEY. Correct.

GRACE. Is that just me or anybody in my family?

MARKLEY. Your entire family. It precludes a wrongful-death action also.

GRACE *(looks at the paper again)*. This is a confidential settlement.

MARKLEY. Yes.

GRACE. You didn't say nothin' about it being confidential.

MARKLEY. That's standard for most legal settlements, Miss Fryer. We like to protect our privacy. And your privacy also. It cuts both ways. You agree to keep silent about the terms of the settlement, and so do we.

MRS. FRYER. That seems fair.

MARKLEY. Need a pen? *(MARKLEY takes out a pen, hands it to GRACE. She takes it, looks back at the pages.)*

GRACE. I have another question.

MRS. FRYER. Grace. Mr. Markley already explained the settlement to you.

GRACE. Ma.

MARKLEY. I don't mind.

GRACE. What is contributory negligence, Mr. Markley? *(MARKLEY is puzzled. He looks at the document.)* It's not in that one. It was in them other papers. That you filed. When we did the lawsuit. The radium company said its defense was the statute of limitations and contributory negligence.

MARKLEY. I'm not sure what you're asking, Miss Fryer.

GRACE. It means it's our fault. Don't it?

MARKLEY. It's a standard defense, Miss Fryer. I wouldn't take it personally.

GRACE. How else can I take it?

MRS. FRYER. Mr. Markley. Grace has had an awful headache all day. Maybe you could leave the papers—

GRACE. Maybe he can just answer the question.

MRS. FRYER. Why are you doing this?

GRACE. Why didn't you tell me Miss Wiley was here?

MRS. FRYER. You already made up your mind. She'd only try to talk you out of it.

GRACE. What did she say about Kathryn?

MRS. FRYER. Mr. Markley, if you'll leave the papers, Grace will sign them later.

GRACE. Ma! What did she say about Kathryn?

MRS. FRYER. She said. It don't look good. *(A moment.)*

MARKLEY. Perhaps I should come back later, when Miss Fryer is feeling better.

GRACE. You didn't answer my question, Mr. Markley. And I'd really like an answer. Because, let me tell you: I quit school at fifteen! I went to work at the radium plant because my folks needed the money. At your factory, they told us what to do. When to do it. How to do it. My folks didn't raise me to make trouble. So I didn't make trouble. I did what I was told. I never asked questions! How do you get contributory negligence out of that?

MARKLEY. As I said, it's a standard defense.

GRACE. There's nothin' standard about what happened to me.

True Stories Told in Scenes and Monologues | 79

MARKLEY. We deeply regret your situation. But there is no evidence to tie your condition to any actions by the U.S. Radium Corporation.

GRACE. Then why are you givin' me this money?

MARKLEY. It's … it's a humanitarian gesture.

GRACE *(laughs)*. A humanitarian gesture?

MRS. FRYER. Mr. Markley. I'll take them papers.

GRACE *(blocking her)*. Humanitarian! Month after month you put us off! Delay after delay. Knowin' how sick we were. How tired. And desperate. Humanitarian! You're waiting for us to die!

MRS. FRYER *(confidentially)*. Grace. Please. Stop this now.

GRACE. Ma. One by one, I watched my friends get sick. And die. In the most horrible way. And you think I should be grateful? For any spare change they throw at me?

MARKLEY. Miss Fryer. This is a very generous offer, under the circumstances. I would advise you to take it. Because it won't be on the table very long.

MRS. FRYER. What do you mean?

MARKLEY. If Miss Fryer does not sign within twenty-four hours, we will be forced to withdraw our offer. Permanently.

MRS. FRYER. Grace.

GRACE. He's lying.

MARKLEY. I beg your pardon, miss!

GRACE. You're trying to tell me if I don't sign these now—but I came back a week from now and said I changed my mind, you'd still rather go to court? You'd still rather some judge get a look at me … and take your chances I won't win on sympathy alone? Twenty-four hours. You're just trying to bully me.

MARKLEY. Very well, then. Miss Fryer. I'll take that for a no. And we'll see you in court. *(MARKLEY packs up his briefcase and exits as MRS. FRYER sees him out.)*

GRACE. Yes, you will! You will see me. If they have to carry me in there, you'll see me. You and Mr. Roeder both!

MRS. FRYER. You call that man back.

GRACE. I'm goin' to court, Ma.

MRS. FRYER. What are you trying to prove? You know you can't win!

GRACE. I want those people to look at me! I want them to look at me and explain how it's my fault I got sick working in their factory!

MRS. FRYER. And what will that get ya? What?

GRACE. Ma. All my life, I've done what other people told me to do. I quit school. Because you said I should. I put that brush in my mouth 'cause Mrs. McNeil said I should. I never said, please can't I finish school? I never said, I don't like the taste of this paint. I never argued. Even though I knew—Ma. I knew somethin' wasn't right. At night, I'd lie in bed, and I'd see my dress. Hanging on the back of the closet door. All aglow. My shoes on the floor. My hairbrush. And comb. On the dresser. So much light, Ma. So much light! And I never once questioned. I never once asked! Don't you see? They knew I wouldn't. *That's* what they were counting on.

Black Elk Speaks

Based on the book by John Neihardt
Adapted by Christopher Sergel

In 1862, on the Santee Reservation in Minnesota, Little Crow is visited by two young men who tell him of a misadventure brought on by their own poor judgment. Little Crow quickly realizes the unavoidable ramifications: once again, settlers and natives will do battle, and it will not go well for his people.

LITTLE CROW
SHAKOPEE
MEDICINE BOTTLE

***

LITTLE CROW. Why are you here?

SHAKOPEE. Some young men of my band were hungry. We crossed the river to hunt in the Big Woods, because we were very hungry. *[(The SPIRIT GUIDE sounds the rattle again.)]*

LITTLE CROW. Go on.

SHAKOPEE. Something happened.

MEDICINE BOTTLE. We came to a settler's fence; I found a hen's nest with some eggs.

SHAKOPEE. I warned him, don't take the eggs …

MEDICINE BOTTLE *(with contempt)* … they belong to the white man.

SHAKOPEE. He called me a coward! *[(The SPIRIT GUIDE sounds a sustained rattle.)]*

LITTLE CROW. And what did you do to prove you are not a coward?

SHAKOPEE. I asked if he was brave enough to go up to the house with me while I shot the white man. He said …

MEDICINE BOTTLE. I said we'd see who is braver.

LITTLE CROW. The others with you, they decided to be brave too?

MEDICINE BOTTLE. We all went after them. *(Proudly displaying five newly-taken scalps.)* We killed three men and two women. *([The rattle stops as the SPIRIT GUIDE "takes" five "shots" created by five strikes of the drum.] Silence. It's even worse than LITTLE CROW expected.)*

LITTLE CROW. And two women?

MEDICINE BOTTLE. Then we took their wagon and drove back to camp to tell what we had done. *(LITTLE CROW looks at them, utterly horrified. It's a moment before he can speak.)*

LITTLE CROW. It must be a very big wagon to carry all the punishment, suffering, death you've brought back to the Santee.

SHAKOPEE. It is a question of manhood.

LITTLE CROW. So you killed two women? My congratulations. But why tell your heroic exploits to me? Go talk to Traveling Hail.

SHAKOPEE. You're our chief, we need your experience. *(LITTLE CROW cannot suppress a grim ironic laugh.)*

LITTLE CROW. It's almost dawn. We should start appreciating every new dawn we see.

SHAKOPEE. Instead of waiting for the soldiers to come kill us, let's strike first!

MEDICINE BOTTLE. Now! While they're fighting among themselves to the south.

LITTLE CROW. No.

SHAKOPEE. With women killed, they'll take a dreadful vengeance.

LITTLE CROW. You are right.

SHAKOPEE. We have no choice.

LITTLE CROW. We do. We can accept their vengeance.

SHAKOPEE *(stunned)*. In place of fighting?

LITTLE CROW. In place of extermination.

MEDICINE BOTTLE *(the VOICE we've heard before, but now a direct taunt)*. Kangi' ci' k'ala is a coward! *[(At this challenge, the SPIRIT GUIDE sounds the rattle and rushes frantically around LITTLE CROW.)]* COWARD!

(MEDICINE BOTTLE produces a knife for the "to-the-death" fight that must follow. [The rattle stops.])

LITTLE CROW. This terrible word … coward. Is this word worth the lives of all the young men who are going to die for it? *[(The rattle stops.)]* Is it?

(MEDICINE BOTTLE and SHAKOPEE are confused that LITTLE CROW has not answered the challenge.)

LITTLE CROW *(cont't)*. You are like little dogs in the Hot Moon when they run mad and snap at their shadows. Open your eyes and try to see. The white men are like the snow when the sky is a blizzard. You may kill one-two-ten; yes, as many as the leaves in the forest, and their brothers will not miss them. Kill one-two-ten, and ten times ten will come to kill you. Count your fingers all day long and white men with guns will come faster than you can count.

SHAKOPEE. If we fight bravely ...

LITTLE CROW. Talk bravery into the mouth of a cannon! You're fools.

SHAKOPEE. What should we do?

LITTLE CROW *([rattle sounds.] Considers for a moment. There are no options)*. There is only one thing you can do. Go, string your bows, make arrows, prepare for war ... *(His voice chokes off.)*

SHAKOPEE. What will you do?

(Rattle out. The SPIRIT GUIDE freezes.)

LITTLE CROW. Kangi' ci' k'ala is also a fool. Kangi' ci' k'ala will die with you.

Looking for Roberto Clemente

Book and lyrics by Karen Zacarías
Music by Deborah Wicks La Puma

It's 1972. Legendary baseball star Roberto Clemente has stepped up to the plate, and as he goes for his 3,000th hit, young fan Sam Kowalski is at home, listening to the game on radio. But wait! Something in the airwaves has made it possible for Roberto to hear what Sam is saying—and for Sam to hear Roberto!

ANNOUNCER
SAM
CLEMENTE

***

ANNOUNCER. Two outs and the bases full of runners as Roberto Clemente steps up to the plate. Will this be his 3,000th hit?

SAM. Come on number 21!

ANNOUNCER. He swings. Strike one!

SAM. Come on, Roberto!

ANNOUNCER. The wind up, the pitch. Strike two!

(SAM is in agony.)

ANNOUNCER *(cont'd)*. "The Great One" is down two nothing in the count and here it comes … and … *(Sound of bat hitting ball.)* Foul ball. The crowd is on its feet begging for that 3,000th hit. *(Crowd cheers.)* Clemente checks his swing. He's ready for the pitch … but wait, he steps out of the box …

SAM. Listen to me, Roberto, calm down.

CLEMENTE. Calm down …

SAM. Hold your bat tight.

CLEMENTE. Hold my bat tight.

SAM. And hit one for me!

ANNOUNCER. The wind up … the pitch … and—*(CRACK!)* Open up the windows Aunt Millie, it's coming through!

SAM. You did it! 3,000!

ANNOUNCER. It's 1972 and Roberto Clemente has hit 3,000! And it looks like a DOUBLE! A DOUBLE! But wait … the ball is still going,

going, downtown ... way out of the outfield ... further and further ... down the street ... turning the corner? This ball is long gone!

(ROBERTO runs the bases. SAM is jumping up and down with joy.)

CLEMENTE *(while running)*. Thank you! Gracias!
SAM. You're welcome!
CLEMENTE. I couldn't have done it without you.
SAM. Don't mention it, Bob!
CLEMENTE. My name is Roberto, not Bob.

(Note: Although CLEMENTE and SAM connect through the radio, at no time are they directly present in each other's space.)

SAM. Sorry, Roberto! Whoa! Wait, can you hear me?
CLEMENTE. Can you hear me? All I ask is you call me by my real name.
SAM. You can hear me! I can't believe this! I'm talking to Roberto Clemente. Hi! I'm Sam Kowalski. You're my hero.
CLEMENTE. Hero?
SAM. Yes! Twelve Gold Glove Awards, 1971 World Series champion and MVP with a series batting average of .414. Plus you've smashed 22 of your batting helmets.
CLEMENTE. I feel baseball strongly.
SAM. I love baseball too.
CLEMENTE. What position you play?
SAM. Me? Oh, I don't play. Not really. I'm not on a team. It would be nice to be on a team. I mean if someone wanted me on their team ... but, you know ... nobody does. I get so nervous. I sweat ... I'm, like, the clutch player that has no clutch. When it really matters, I, like, really lose. But still, I looooove baseball.
CLEMENTE. To love what you do ... is very important. I play every game, like my life depends on it.
SAM. Holy moley, if only I could take a picture of this, of us, just talking on the ... radio ...

[(Crowd chants: CLEMENTE! CLEMENTE! ...)]

CLEMENTE. Sam, *amigo*, I have to go ...
SAM. Wait!
CLEMENTE. *Silencio! (The fans go silent.)* Yes?

SAM *(beat)*. How do you do it?

(Pause.)

CLEMENTE. I don't know. How does a seed reach the sky?
SAM. Huh?

[(Crowd chants again: CLEMENTE! CLEMENTE! ...)]

ANNOUNCER. And Roberto waves to his fans and …

(Radio starts to fizz out ... SAM turns the dials ...)

SAM. Oh, no, I'm losing the signal … Can you hear me? *(The radio sputters.)* Wait, don't go—*(Beat.)* Lost him. Whatchagonnado?

In the Garden of Live Flowers:
A Fantasia on the Life and Work of Rachel Carson
By Attilio Favorini and Lynne Conner

In the early 1960s, Rachel Carson faces battles on several fronts. Charged with the support of her extended family, diagnosed with breast cancer and facing increasing opposition from chemical corporations, she struggles to complete her book, *Silent Spring*, meant to awaken the world to growing ecological dangers. She finds support at a meeting with her literary agent Marie Rodell in the office of Wallace Shawn, editor of *New Yorker* magazine.

RACHEL
SHAWN
MARIE RODELL

***

RACHEL *(shaking his hand)*. Mr. Shawn.

SHAWN. Didn't I just overhear the words "chemical company"? *(To MARIE RODELL.)* I assume you just told her the news about Velsicol?

RACHEL *(interrupting)*. What's happening with Velsicol?

SHAWN. You know the name?

RACHEL. Of course I do. They're the sole manufacturers of chlordane and heptachlor.

SHAWN. Our lawyer received a phone call from their general counsel insinuating a suit unless we cancel the June 30th excerpt.

RACHEL. Because I allude to the dangers of those chemicals?

SHAWN. He's accusing you of libel. He's saying there's no scientific evidence that Velsicol's products are dangerous.

RACHEL. That's a pack of wretched lies. *(To MARIE.)* I won't settle for it.

SHAWN. Certainly not, Miss Carson. We told the lawyer to go ahead and sue. We stand by your book's fair and accurate analysis.

MARIE RODELL. But, Rachel, there's more. This morning I heard from the editor of *Audubon* magazine. It seems the Velsicol lawyers treated him to lunch and a host of threats about the safety of his personal financial future—were he to insist on publishing excerpts of …

RACHEL *(interrupting her)*. Have they threatened Houghton Mifflin?

MARIE RODELL. Yes.

RACHEL. Will we still come out on time?

SHAWN. Houghton won't knuckle under. The book will come out in the fall on schedule—assuming you finish the chapter on biological control.

RACHEL. I am ... I will. Very shortly. You know I don't like to miss my deadlines. It's just there have been a few interruptions of late ...

MARIE RODELL. She's taking care of it, Mr. Shawn. She'll have the finished draft by the end of the month.

SHAWN. Not to pressure you, Miss Carson. You have my utmost esteem, as always. The point of this meeting is to prepare you for a very difficult battle ahead. Believe me when I tell you that Velsicol is not the only chemical company on the war path.

MARIE RODELL. Rachel, are you ... Do you really think you have enough energy to fight this now?

SHAWN. Enough energy? For the whirlwind that is Miss Carson? *(Pause.)* Is there something amiss?

RACHEL *(quickly)*. Marie is just worried about my ongoing family obligations. That's all. She's just concerned about how I'm going to manage Roger's care now that my mother is gone and there's so much traveling to do.

SHAWN *(with courtly pity)*. How is the boy? He misses his great-grandmother, surely.

RACHEL. He's fine. He's had more than his share of loss, of course. But he knows how much I love him. *(Looking directly and defiantly at MARIE RODELL.)* And he knows that his great-auntie Rachel will always be here to take care of him.

SHAWN. You are a great comfort to him, I've no doubt.

RACHEL. I appreciate your concern. *(To MARIE RODELL.)* Both of you. *(Stiffening.)* Nevertheless, I have to say I'm a little disappointed in the tone of this meeting. I thought I was here to bask in your approval and delight.

SHAWN *(over MARIE RODELL's speech below)*. Do forgive me, Miss Carson. The response to the chapters we've included in *Reporter at Large* is overwhelming. Absolutely overwhelming.

MARIE RODELL *(over SHAWN's speech)*. Darling Rachel, of course I'm proud and excited. It *is* over whelming. Truly. I've confirmed the Eric Sevareid interview for "CBS Reports." They'll film from your house. OK?

RACHEL *(touching her wig)*. All right.

MARIE RODELL. And I've also confirmed with Secretary Udall. You're to be President Kennedy's honored guest at the White House Conference on Conservation.

SHAWN. This is surely your proudest moment, Miss Carson. It's true, you know, what Justice Douglas wrote about *Silent Spring*: It is the most revolutionary book since *Uncle Tom's Cabin*.

MARIE RODELL. You are gaining some extraordinary fans these days, aren't you?

SHAWN *(pulls a letter from his jacket pocket)*. On the topic of fans, I wanted to share a piece of mail with you both. One of our secretaries singled it out for reasons that will become obvious. *(Opening up the letter and reading.)* "June 23, 1962. Miss Rachel Carson's reference to the selfishness of insecticide manufacturers probably reflects her communist sympathies, like a lot of our writers today. We can live without birds and animals, but, as the current market slump shows, we cannot live without business. As for insects, isn't it just like a woman to be scared to death of a few little bugs! As long as we have the H-bomb every thing will be OK. P.S. She's probably a peace-nut too." *(Rachel stares at SHAWN. General silence.)*

MARIE RODELL. A crackpot. We'll just file it under "C."

RACHEL *(takes the letter from SHAWN, reads silently, and then aloud)*. "Scared to death of a few little bugs." I'll show them "just like a woman."

OTHER PLAYS OF INTEREST

Not all plays offer monologues, duets or trios that will stand on their own. This in no way reflects on the quality of the play or the importance of its story. If you are interested in full scripts dealing with American historical events and notable people, here are additional titles you might like to consider. All are available from Dramatic Publishing Company. It should also be noted that these scripts, and the ones from which the excerpts were taken for this anthology, may also contain scenes for four or more actors that can stand on their own for study or performance purposes. Please remember that all performances must be licensed through the publisher.

Bird Woman: The Story of Sacagawea
    By Ric Averill

Civil War Voices
    By James R. Harris, featuring songs of the period with arrangements by Mark Hayes.

The Fastest Woman Alive
    By Karen Sunde

Four Little Girls: Birmingham 1963
    By Christina M. Ham

The Heavens Are Hung in Black
    By James Still

A Laura Ingalls Wilder Christmas
    By Laurie Brooks

Leaving Hannibal
    By Mary Collins Barile

Lincoln's Log or Better Angels
    By Barry Kornhauser

Mean To Be Free: A Flight North on the Underground Railroad
    By Joanna H. Kraus

Mr. Clemens and Mr. Brown
    By Sally Netzel

Ms. Courageous: Women of Science
    By Joanna H. Kraus

My Days as a Youngling - John Jacob Niles: The Early Years
    Adapted and scripted by Nancy Niles Sexton, Vaughn McBride & Martha Harrison Jones, songs composed by John Jacob Niles

Nevermore! Edgar Allan Poe, the Final Mystery
    By Julian Wiles

POE! POE! POE! The Life and Writings of Edgar Allan Poe
    By Kathryn Schultz Miller

The Rebel: Johnny Yuma at Appomattox
    By Andrew J. Fenady

To Life! Growing Up Jewish in America
    By Sandra Fenichel Asher

Sojourner Truth Is My Name
    By Pat Sternberg and Dolly Beechman

TOTTY: Young Eleanor Roosevelt
    By Sharon Whitney

Walk, Don't Ride! A Celebration of the Fight for Equality
    By Peter Manos

We Will Remember: A Tribute to Veterans
    By Sandra Fenichel Asher

A Woman Called Truth
    By Sandra Fenichel Asher

The Yellow Boat
    By David Saar

NOTES

NOTES

NOTES

NOTES